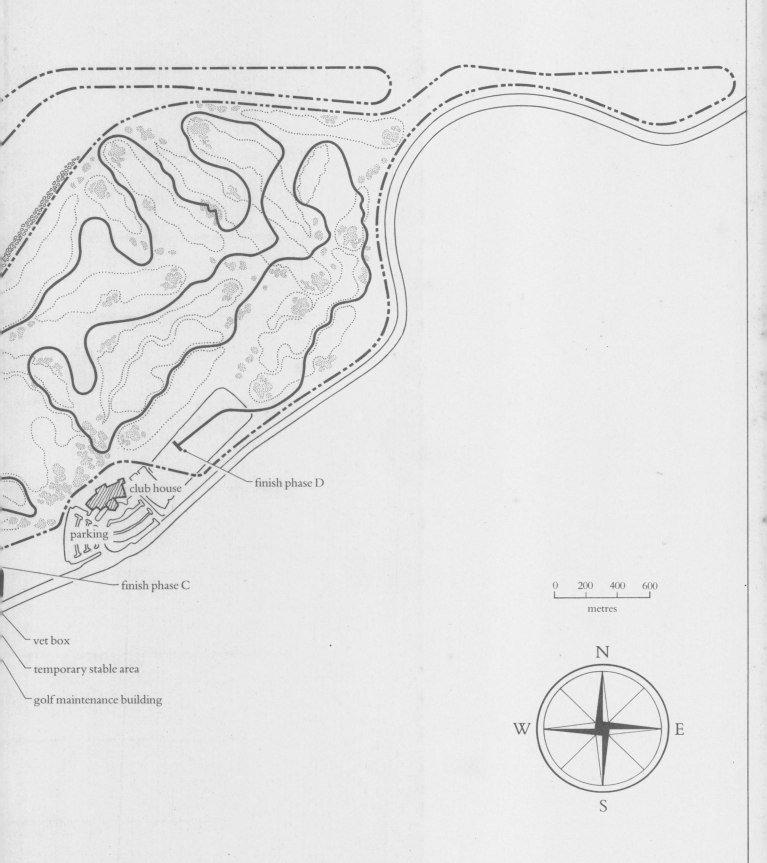

club house

finish phase D

parking

finish phase C

vet box

temporary stable area

golf maintenance building

0   200   400   600

metres

N

W   E

S

# The SR Direct Mail Book of EVENTING

## Alan Smith and Brian Giles

**Stanley Paul**

London Melbourne Sydney Auckland Johannesburg

Stanley Paul & Co. Ltd

An imprint of the Hutchinson Publishing Group
17–21 Conway Street, London W1P 6JD

Hutchinson Publishing Group (Australia) Pty Ltd
PO Box 496, 16–22 Church Street, Hawthorne, Melbourne, Victoria 3122

Hutchinson Group (NZ) Ltd
32–34 View Road, PO Box 40–486, Glenfield, Auckland 10

Hutchinson Group (SA) (Pty) Ltd
PO Box 337, Bergvlei 2012, South Africa

First published 1984
© Brian Giles and Alan Smith 1984

Set in Bembo

Printed in Great Britain by Jolly & Barber Ltd, Rugby
Bound by Anchor Brendon Ltd, Tiptree, Essex

British Library Cataloguing in Publication Data
Giles, Brian
  The SR direct mail book of eventing
  1. Eventing (Horsemanship)
  I. Title
  798.2´4      SF295.7
       ISBN 0 09 155180 3

Frontispiece: *Nils Haagensen and Monaco, European
champions in 1979 and winners of the Fontainebleau Festival in
1980, over the Slide at Badminton*

# Contents

# What is Direct Mail?

Direct Mail advertising is quite simply advertising your product or service through the medium of the postal system. Advertising literature is collated into envelopes and sent directly to the individuals that make up the appropriate target audience.

This form of advertising (more widely known as direct marketing) puts the advertiser in direct contact with the potential client, and is one of the few forms that allows the user directly to link the cost of an advertising campaign to response or increased sales.

John Burbidge, the chairman of SR Direct Mail, whose head office is based at Blackhorse Road, Deptford, is a man who believes totally in taking part in whatever sport his company backs.

He sponsors Lucinda Green and her husband David; puts up the money for an all-important Newcomers show-jumping competition, and supplies the backing for individual shows and classes. He has done a great deal for equestrian sport.

And, in a short time, he has put the world of direct mailing into the homes of millions – not only by posting them the information – but also by having his company name in practically every newspaper in the land when Lucinda won Badminton for a record five times.

Win or lose, he knows what his riders are feeling because he also competes himself, in hunter trials.

'I find riding a great release from the pressures of business,' he says, 'and whenever I can spare the time to ride for pleasure, or compete, I do.'

Just to say that John Burbidge and his company put money into sport would be a gross understatement, because he is also a highly efficient businessman, with good ideas and, after starting SR Direct Mail with a £50,000 mortgage, it now turns over nearly £7 million a year, with associated companies.

The next step is to go public, a dream which is likely to become reality for a man whose motto is 'Tomorrow won't do'.

# Acknowledgements

Our special thanks to all of those riders and officials – from Britain and overseas – who helped in the preparation of this book; to Janet Dry and Pamela Crosher who typed it, to Judith Draper who read it and to Marion Paull who edited it.

# An Introduction to Eventing

The sport of horse trials, or eventing, is designed to test the all-round training and fitness of the horse and although to the uninitiated the format seems complicated and hard to grasp – how often in the non-equestrian press has HRH Princess Anne, a former European Horse Trials Champion, been referred to as a 'show jumper'! – in reality it is quite simple, all events comprising three phases: dressage, speed and endurance including cross-country, and show jumping.

The simplest form of horse trials, the one-day event, begins with dressage, followed by show jumping and then the cross-country. The two-day event, which provides a useful stepping stone for those wishing to participate in full-scale trials such as Badminton or Burghley, follows the same pattern, but usually includes some roads and tracks and a short steeplechase as well as the cross-country. The top-level three-day event devotes a day to each phase, beginning with dressage on day one, followed by the speed and endurance and cross-country on day two, and show jumping on day three. However, nowadays these major events attract so many entries that it is usually necessary to run them over four days rather than three, the dressage tests occupying the first two days.

Although anyone can, in theory, organise horse trials – riding clubs and Pony Club branches, for instance, often run 'unofficial' ones for their members – riders who wish to event seriously will want to compete at 'official' trials, that is those affiliated to the national governing body of the sport, the British Horse Society. BHS horse trials are staged throughout the country during the spring and autumn and cater for all grades of horses, from novice up to advanced level. To compete at official national events riders must belong to the BHS and also to its Horse Trials Group, and their horses must be registered with the Society. International events are run under the rules of the *Fédération Equestre Internationale* (FEI), the sport's overall governing body to which all the national federations are affiliated.

The first step on the eventing ladder is the novice one-day event, 'novice' referring to the horse. Horses are graded according to experience. A win or a place in an event earns a horse points and when a certain total (as specified by the BHS) is reached, the horse then moves into the next grade. Thus the novice horse gradually goes on to compete at intermediate and, eventually, advanced level. This points system ensures that horses progress gradually from novice to more difficult competitions, without the risk of being overfaced by over-eager riders.

For the uninitiated the judging of the dressage test undoubtedly presents the most problems and it cannot be denied that it is quite a complicated business. In any one event each horse is required to perform the same pre-determined test. A test for the novice horse lasts about four and a half minutes and the movements are simple and straightforward. Tests become progressively longer and more difficult as the horse moves up the grade system until at international level a horse will be in the arena for some seven and a half minutes and will be required to perform more advanced movements such as the half-pass.

The number of judges varies from perhaps just one at novice trials to three for a big international event, and each movement of the test is marked by each judge on a scale of from 0–10: a score of '0' would indicate that the horse failed to perform the required movement; '10' would mean that the movement was 'excellent'. Each judge is also allowed to award a further 4 marks on the 0–10 scale for overall impression, which includes freedom and regularity of the horse's paces, impulsion and submission on the part of the horse, and the correctness or otherwise of the rider's position, seat and application of the aids.

As an example, at the Badminton three-day event, where the dressage test itself comprises 20 movements, the maximum possible score for each competitor would be $200 + 40 = 240$ marks.

Should horse and rider exceed the optimum time for the test or make an error, of course, penalties are awarded. At the end of the test each judge's marks are totalled and any penalties deducted. All the judges' 'good' marks are then totalled and averaged, and the resultant figure is deducted from the total possible score. A multiplying factor is then applied to give a final score in penalty points. This multiplying factor depends upon the severity of the cross-country course; if it is considered a hard one, the multiplying factor will be high, if easy it will be low. This is because in every three-day event the relative influence of the three phases should be in the

*Dressage, always the first phase of a three-day event. Ginny Holgate on Priceless*

*After the dressage, the steeplechase, demonstrated here by Goran Breisner on Ultimus . . .*

ratio of dressage 3, speed and endurance (including the cross-country) 12, show jumping 1. The assessment of the cross-country course is made by the ground jury; obviously it would be easier for them to do this when the cross-country had been completed, but if they waited that long no one would know the precise dressage scores until after the second phase; so they have to make a judgement. At a major three-day event such as Burghley, a score in the region of 30–40 penalty points would be very good.

The speed and endurance is much easier to follow as far as scoring is concerned. Straightforward penalties are awarded for refusals, falls and for exceeding the

*. . . then the roads and tracks, Australian Merv Bennett . . .*

*. . . and a quick rub down before . . .*

*. . . the cross-country, David Green and Super Salesman . . .*

optimum time, and these are simply totalled and then added to the dressage score. While this phase at one-day events simply comprises a cross-country course, varying in length from about one and a half to two and a half miles, depending on the standard of the event (novice, intermediate, etc.), in a full three-day event there are in fact four sections on what is commonly referred to as 'cross-country' day.

Phases A and C, roads and tracks, and Phase B, the steeplechase, generally attract little public attention, but they can have a significant effect upon the individual competitor's overall performance. The length of these phases varies with the standard of competition, European, World and Olympic Championships obviously being the most demanding.

At a normal three-day event the first roads and tracks section might be about three miles, which must be completed within a stipulated time. This will normally be negotiated mainly at trot and the rider needs to keep a close eye on the time to avoid incurring time penalties.

*. . .followed by the final show-jumping phase. Rachel Bayliss and Mystic Minstrel, winners of the 1983 European Championship*

Above: *The first ever winner of Gatcombe (1983) – David Green and runner-up Lucinda Green, after being divided from a dead-heat by dressage marks*

Equally, there is nothing to be gained by completing this phase much faster than is required – this will merely tire the horse unnecessarily.

The steeplechase follows immediately, the course being between approximately one and two miles in length, again depending on the standard of the event. The horse has to negotiate about 10 brush fences of the type seen at point-to-points – in some overseas events the fences are more unusual – and must take them at a fair gallop to complete the course within the allotted time. A fall at a steeplechase obstacle incurs the same penalties as one on the cross-country course (60 penalties).

Next comes Phase C, the second roads and tracks section, which is usually about twice as long as Phase A. Again, careful timing is of the essence. There is no benefit in finishing early – it will probably mean that the rider has taken more out of the horse than is necessary which could cause problems on the last phase, the cross-country. Riders are permitted to dismount and run beside their horses during the roads and tracks phase and those who are fit enough usually take advantage of this opportunity to take the weight off their horses' backs.

After Phase C comes an obligatory ten-minute halt during which the horse undergoes a veterinary inspection to determine its fitness to continue with the cross-country. If the horse is considered unfit to go on it is compulsorily withdrawn – colloquially known as being 'spun' – from the event.

The most popular phase with spectators and for the majority of the riders is the cross-country, in which at three-day-event level horses jump upwards of 30 fences of every conceivable variation, over different types of natural terrain. The distance covered will be in the region of four and a half miles and the course takes around ten minutes to complete. Again riders must aim to complete it within the optimum time if they are not to incur time penalties.

On the cross-country course penalties are awarded as follows: first refusal, run-out or circle at an obstacle – 20 penalties; second refusal, run-out or circle at the same obstacle – 40 penalties; third refusal, run-out or circle at the same obstacle – elimination; fall of horse or rider within the prescribed 'penalty zone' of an obstacle – 60 penalties; error of course – elimination.

At the end of the speed and endurance, penalties, including any time penalties incurred in any of the various phases, are totalled and added to the dressage penalties. Horses who are passed fit by the vets on the last day take part in the final show-jumping phase, which is designed to test the suppleness and obedience of the animals following the rigours of the previous day. It has become customary on the last day of three-day events for competitors to jump in reverse order of merit, those with the best scores going last. It is a good ploy for building up tension among spectators and ensuring that the event finishes on an exciting note.

Penalties in the show jumping are awarded as follows: fence knocked down or fault at water jump – 5 penalties; first disobedience (refusal, run-out, etc) – 10 penalties; second disobedience – 20 penalties; third disobedience – elimination; fall of horse or rider – 30 penalties; error of course – elimination. Time penalties are given for exceeding the time allowed (0.25 penalty for each second over the time), and elimination ensues for exceeding the time limit (twice the time allowed). Unlike the cross-country phase, where refusals are cumulative at one fence, in the show jumping competitors are allowed only two disobediences over the entire course.

Any penalties incurred in the show jumping are added to those brought forward from the dressage and speed and endurance sections, which usually produces a clear winner. In the unusual event of two or more riders finishing on equal scores the winner is the one with the best cross-country score. If there is still equality, the dressage scores are used to divide competitors – the competitor with the most 'good' marks being declared the winner.

# 1
# Man in the Hot Seat

Chris Collins, chairman of the British Horse Trials Selection Committee, brings to the job precisely those qualities that have made him, in his early forties, such a successful businessman. 'Money, determination and talent' are his recipe for reaching the top of international eventing every bit as much as in business, and determination is the one he rates most highly. The merits of these qualities are abundantly proved by the British team's results.

'Very few people have all three of the qualities, but two are enough to produce the third. If you've got determination and talent then you eventually get successful: money and determination will get you quite a long way. Probably talent and money might be the weakest. That's an over-simplification, of course, for there are several ingredients to success, but an extremely important one is determination.'

That is what he looks for in potential international riders, and what has marked his own life, both in business and sport. Chris Collins started his sporting life in racing, and it still occupies a great deal of his time and attention, as a steward of the Jockey Club, member of various committees of the Club, and of the Horserace Betting Levy Board.

He was brought up in the Buckinghamshire countryside where he still lives: his mother rode but his father was not much interested. 'My father was rather against it. He was happy enough for me to ride when I was at school, but he was always worried that I wouldn't work – that it would seduce me.' Mr Collins senior was reckoning without the drive that carried Chris to the

top of the amateur riders' table and has enabled him to build up a couple of very promising businesses, as well as his demanding committee work.

He started riding at about twelve – 'very unremarkably in the Pony Club' – but became 'totally absorbed' in racing. He started in point-to-points and then, after a lot of reversals, went on to National Hunt racing proper, but all the time suffering from a problem that in his chosen sport is almost an insuperable one: 'I am just too heavy.' Chris Collins stands over 6ft high and is heavily built, and throughout his racing career had a battle with the scales.

He qualified as an accountant in 1965, aged twenty-five, and for the next two and a half years devoted himself almost full time to racing. Before that year's Grand National he had bought a horse, Mr Jones, from County Durham trainer Arthur Stephenson because he thought that 'this might be the only opportunity for me ever to ride in it.' This came about because that great horse Mill House, who had been top weight for the race, was taken out, and the other weights automatically were raised. Collins and Mr Jones finished third, and that was enough for him to forsake almost everything else and concentrate on riding in racing.

Having reached this decision, he also decided that Arthur Stephenson should be the man to go to. He had met Stephenson through BBC television commentator Julian Wilson, when looking for a Grand National horse, and was 'very impressed with him. Some amateurs from outside racing get taken literally for a ride by their trainers but I was sure he would not do that.

And I thought it would be better for me to go north and get down to it.'

'Get down to it' he certainly did, living for the first winter at a nearby pub, riding out three lots every morning and going racing in the afternoons. 'And when I did not go racing I'd go to the Turkish baths.'

During his racing career Chris Collins reached the pinnacle not only in Britain, but abroad as well, winning the Swedish Grand National and the famous Pardubice Steeplechase in Czechoslovakia, widely rated as the toughest in the world, even more hazardous than the Grand National at Aintree. Collins was the first Englishman ever to win it.

*Before eventing and selection, Chris Collins was a champion amateur jockey, here on Credit Call*

But his good times had to come to an end, and that end came suddenly. 'I had four falls in the space of a week,' he recalls. 'In the first I broke my nose and compressed a few vertebrae – that shook me up. I went on riding, and had a winner, but on the Saturday I had a fall, and another on the Monday, and on the Wednesday I had another bad fall, and broke my arm very badly.'

Even the determined Mr Collins could not carry on race-riding with a broken arm. Ted Edgar once rode round Hickstead with his arm in plaster, but the Jockey Club does not approve of such heroics and he was grounded for the next six months.

Although it was a drastic way of getting his mind back on to business it could not have happened at a more opportune time. His father had started the Goya perfumery business, but had sold it in 1961 to Reckitt,

Colman, while remaining on the board; 'but the business had,' said Chris, 'gone downhill, so that in 1968 my father suggested, almost jokingly, that they should sell it back to us, and they did.

'By that time he had bought Suttons Seeds, so I came in to manage Goya.' It was a somewhat unexpected new venture, but one for which he was fully prepared, for in addition to his accountancy he had, while Goya was still a family concern, gone to the French town of Grasse, the Mecca of the perfumery industry. 'I'd rather written that off, except that it had been very good for my French,' he says. He was able to put it to such good account that the ailing company took on a new lease of life, and in 1975 he sold Goya again, this time to ICI.

The spring after breaking his arm he was back racing, but had a most unsuccessful time in hunter chases and thought to himself, 'At twenty-nine I'm too old to start again. It's the desk for you for the rest of your life.'

Chris Collins is far from unhappy behind a desk. Many active men may feel claustrophobic in such circumstances, but he enjoys it, the planning and dealing that goes on in the life of an entrepreneur. However, he certainly did not want to give up competitive riding, and looked around for other avenues. 'I didn't know anything about eventing or show jumping, but I was talking to Johnny Kidd and said I was thinking of taking up another sport. He said, "Don't try show jumping, it's too professional, you won't get anywhere. Eventing is your sport." And that seemed to make absolute sense to me – I was attracted to the cross-country as the closest to racing.'

Johnny Kidd, himself a former successful show-jumping rider and now polo player, could not have given better advice, but where and how to break this new ground? The answer appeared on television, for Chris had seen Richard Walker win Badminton on Pasha, in 1969, and knew he was trained by Lars Seder-holm, the Swedish-born rider-turned-trainer, who has established himself at Waterstock, Oxfordshire, only a short drive from Collins' home. He arranged to go there in 1969 – and stayed for several years.

'Ironically, although my eventing was very unsuccessful for a few years, the training did give a shot in the arm to my racing, and gave me more of the horsemanship I needed, especially with younger horses. So it was paying off, and I enjoyed it.' Paying off it was, indeed, for it was during this period that he won the Swedish National in 1973 on Hilbirio, and the Pardubice with Stephen's Society the following year.

Perhaps it was because he was so often in the winner's enclosure on the racecourse that, in retrospect, he regards his eventing career as 'a narrow failure'. He had

been looking for the same sort of results, and wanted them quickly. 'I felt I must get to Badminton as fast as possible. I took up eventing in the autumn, and rode at Badminton the following spring. Of course, things were much easier in those days.'

His first events were on an 'old schoolmaster' called Tawny Port, who had already been round Badminton. 'The first two Badmintons I was always number three to jump on the third day, after I'd had some sort of silly fall, but then Centurion came along, who went well. He was eleventh in 1982, and Martin Whiteley, the then chairman of the Selectors, rang up and said would I lend him for the Olympics, to which I said, "No".

'I'd set out in eventing to try and succeed in the same way as I had in steeplechasing, and it would be a positive "minus" to have lent him. It wouldn't have taught me anything and there would have been a risk of the horse being injured. Or at least being drained to the bottom. Every three-day event is a major proportion of a horse's life. At the most if they do ten three-day events it will be a lot. So you'd be exhausting ten per cent of his career.

'It was a completely selfish decision, but I had won practically everything in steeplechasing, all the major hunter chases, and I thought I was an able-bodied rider and therefore I regarded it as an insult to ask for my horse. I respected the Selectors, they have to be tough in their job, but I had no hesitation in saying, "No" – I didn't have to think about it.'

The basis of this refusal is consistent with Chris Collins' whole philosophy, and now that he is chairman of the Selectors one thing they do not do is to ask riders to lend their horses for others to partner in Olympic Games or championships.

'My own view is that I think it is an unhealthy thing to do. The top riders all have quite a lot going for them, they've all got big sponsors, with whom they often have quite complex relationships, so if you then put another horse into, say, Richard Meade or Mark Phillips, it's not going to please George Wimpey or Range Rover. And I think it's rather discouraging for the up-and-coming riders if, as soon as they come up with a good horse, the Selectors try to take it away.

'I believe in the law of the development of the good, and survival – capitalism in a way. That the good people will emerge, and get the sponsorship, and learn to look after themselves. The Selectors shouldn't over-govern and function as a welfare state, and look after certain riders. You might also get the wrong horse with the wrong rider; because a horse has gone very well with one rider it doesn't mean he will with another. It is an interventionist policy and not one I should like to execute. So I am personally against it.'

Collins underlined his point by riding Centurion into fourth place at Burghley in 1973, and he also bought what was, with little doubt, his best three-day-event horse, the Irish-bred Smokey VI. At Badminton, 1974, Collins was ninth and tenth on Smokey and Centurion, respectively, and the Selectors showed they bore no ill-will for his previous refusal by inviting him and Smokey to be part of the British team for the World Championships, which took the silver medal behind the United States. Three years later he and Smokey were in the team that won the European Championship, also at Burghley, and he rode Gamble in the silver medal European Championship team in 1979.

Not a career that most people would decry, but in Chris Collins' view, 'a narrow failure. An honourable failure, perhaps, but I did not achieve what I really wanted to achieve. I felt by 1980, when I was forty, that I was getting too many injuries. And it was not likely, if I went on, that I would succeed. I was asked to be chairman of the Selectors, and I felt to turn it down on the grounds that my hat was still in the ring would be rather a hostage to fate. And as I enjoy desk work as much as outdoors it would be silly to have another year and a half in the sport – which was all I had planned, I was becoming a bit clapped-out – and risk a serious head or back injury against the unlikely prospect that I would do better than I had already done. So I accepted the position.'

His appetite for desk work, and planning and building up a business, had been taking another turn as well, for after selling Goya to ICI Chris Collins turned his attention to the wine trade. He has two businesses, one of which, Collins Wines, just deals with the wine trade while the other, a comparatively new venture which opened in 1982, is a wine supermarket in Primrose Hill, in North London, which, if successful, he plans to expand. 'It's a supermarket, but it's an elegant supermarket which extends right from the bottom to the top of the range: its policy is quality and value throughout the spectrum of wines, so if you spend £2 or £100 on a bottle of wine, it's value. You can go there and taste wines. It's value for money but it's not down-market.'

Businesslike himself, he regards most top three-day-event riders in the same light. 'I think the modern event rider is becoming much more professional, and is a kind

*It may be wet, but it's part of the job – Collins in action on Centurion*

*Chris Collins – time for reflection after the dressage at Luhmühlen in 1979. On the right Major Malcolm Wallace makes notes*

of mini-entrepreneur. They've got sponsors, advertising – they have to have them. I think amateurism is a completely outmoded concept now. Horses cost so much to keep, wages for grooms cost so much, so that we are seeing the development of the top three-day-event rider into a much more professional animal. To be consistently at the top you've got to have such a big string of horses, to have a pyramid of horses coming up through. No one can pay for the running of a stable of horses now unless they're very wealthy or sponsored.'

He recognises that it is much harder these days for a rider to make his or her way up the tree. 'The difficulty is that the top riders are so good – and they are in no way complacent but always working with the best trainers, trying to get the best sponsors. It's not like swimming, where you burn out at nineteen. There is not a lot of room at the top, but I think there is talent

around. One obvious person is Ginny Strawson.' Ginny won the European Young Riders' Championship in 1982 and went on to win the senior international in Boekelo, Holland. Chris is a firm supporter of the Young Riders' Championship: 'It's not just the competition itself, but a way of developing riders coming out of juniors. Now they are looked after, and an interest taken in them, with people knowing what's happening to them, and giving them training, until they're twenty-one. Which gives them a better spring-board into the cold, hard adult world.'

He is insistent that it is 'over to the riders to develop their own careers. The Selection Committee should provide a background which is as helpful as possible to this, but try to be as non-interventionist as possible. For instance, we don't want to own horses, and as I've said I wouldn't want to get involved in trying to take someone off a horse to give to another rider.'

Chris Collins is in no doubt about his, and the Selection Committee's, main priority, and that is 'to provide the best possible preparation for the CCIOs' –

Concours Complet International Officiel, the European and World Championships – 'and the Olympic Games.' Whatever conflict of interests there may be, and no matter whose feelings may be hurt.

'For a championship we do believe, above all, in soundness in the horses. Sometimes there have to be compromises, but what we are looking for is sound, young horses. If there was a choice between a sound, young but lesser combination and an older one with an "if", we would always choose the sounder, younger one, even if the rider was less experienced. We would rather do that than send a leading rider and take a gamble on the horse being sound. It's been done in the past and is a risk one wouldn't want to take.'

Following their belief in letting riders run their own careers, the Selection Committee do not try to get too involved in the planning of each individual's campaign until a championship is imminent but sometimes, especially if the championships are early, as for example with the Los Angeles Olympics, or if the horse concerned is already well experienced and perhaps in 'middle age', they may suggest to the rider that his or her horse should miss out Badminton.

'When we are approaching an Olympics it would be speculative in the extreme to consider anyone who had not distinguished themselves at the previous season's championships, or at Badminton, Burghley, or, perhaps, Boekelo. The next spring we might well suggest certain horses should miss Badminton. This can be difficult because we do have the "Badminton wing", who believe in the supremacy of Badminton, but as I see it my job is to do my best, by policy and execution, to win the CCIO, whereas Badminton's purpose is to be the world's greatest three-day event and provide a spectacle for the 200,000 people who go there. There could be a variance under certain circumstances between their aims and mine, but I'm quite clear about my aims.'

There are other complications. 'Of course, the sponsors want their riders in the best shop window: sometimes we may get a sponsor who wants his horse to go to Badminton or Burghley.' But Britain has not yet had to leave a horse at home for this reason.

'When one is in a job one must do *that* job, if necessary in a rather partisan way. It's not for me to balance the requirements of Badminton in the sport versus Los Angeles: my job is Los Angeles.'

# 2
# A Born Leader

Malcolm Wallace, the man who as *chef d'équipe* has led the British event team to so many important triumphs, and under whose guidance they are the reigning World Champions, had his first taste of international eventing with the Irish tricolour on his saddle cloth. Though he retains a tremendous affinity for the country where he spent much of his youth, there is nothing half-hearted about the way Major Wallace, Commanding Officer of the King's Troop, RHA, has welded the British squad into a formidable fighting force.

Both his parents were of Irish descent, but he had a 'perfectly ordinary Pony Club childhood' in Surrey, hunting with the Chiddingfold Farmers, of which his father was for a while chairman, and taking part in Prince Philip Games, Pony Club horse trials and the like. But the Catholic school, Beaumont College, he should have gone to, following in the steps of his elder brothers, closed, and he went to school in Ireland.

'My pa promised me that if I went to school in Ireland I could have a pony of my own there,' and that was enough of a bait. Not that there was much alternative: 'I wasn't down for anywhere else, no school would take me at the drop of a hat, and my uncle who was over in Ireland arranged it. Over I went, and stayed there for four years. I met Edward O'Grady and had tremendous fun; I used to ride out for his father every time we had a day off – he was down in Tipperary – and went racing whenever we could.'

Edward O'Grady, who has followed in his father's footsteps as a highly successful trainer of racehorses, has remained a close friend of Malcolm's, and is godfather

to his young son, Harry. Racing has long been a Wallace passion, and he rode in his first point-to-point as a boy weighing only 7st 7lb: but in Ireland, after he left school, he spent two years in the stable of Colonel Joe Hume Dudgeon, one of that country's greatest trainers, and while he was there Malcolm Wallace concentrated on eventing.

'To start with I was groom for the Irish three-day-event team: great riders they had then in Colonel Joe's stable – Penny Moreton, she had a wonderful horse called Loughlin,' (they were in the Irish team that won the first World Championship, at Burghley, in 1966) '– and I was competing on Colonel Joe's horses in events and combined training – dressage and show jumping – without a great deal of success but having fun, and was on the short-list for the Irish team in 1965 and 1966. My father said it was better to go to Colonel Joe's yard and be a small fish in a big pond than go to a small yard.

'It was a great experience, but I actually started off with the Irish tricolour under my saddle instead of the Union Jack that I am now responsible for.

'But I was always going to do my National Service, and when National Service stopped I still thought I'd go in and do my three years. I left Ireland after two years, when Colonel Joe died, and joined the Army in 1966. To do my three!' He is, of course, still there. 'Though I am not a career soldier. I don't expect to be Major-General Wallace.'

His Army career started with a light gunner regiment in Hong Kong, and could hardly have been more calculated to suit a horse-mad youngster. 'It was quite exciting, because I got the 1967 riots, all the civil unrest there, so I was sort of blooded fairly early on – and haven't done a great deal since!' They were 'two wonderful years in Hong Kong. I ran the polo stables and played polo twice a week. Then I got posted to Germany, the only time I've been there, for fifteen months, running the show jumping and polo stables. And from there to the long equitation course at Melton, and after that to the Troop.'

The King's Troop, Royal Horse Artillery, has a long and honourable connection with three-day eventing in Britain, including Colonel Bill Lithgow, Malcolm Wallace's predecessor as *chef d'équipe* of the event team, and Colonel Frank Weldon, who had numerous successes in the saddle, including an Olympic team gold and individual bronze on Kilbarry in 1956, and has for many years master-minded Badminton. It was a tradition Malcolm Wallace was well-fitted to continue.

It was soon after he joined the Troop that he 'dis-

covered adult eventing. It had just been Pony Club stuff until then' as far as his British experience was concerned. His best horse was Dr Sebastian, which he had as a three-year-old, backed and broke and eventually rode round Badminton, but 'never did anything particularly well'. The one major competition that Malcolm feels, and with reason, that he should have won was the 1973 Midland Bank Open Championship at Cirencester, but, as he recalls, 'the bloody clock broke down'.

There was not much that could have been done about it, and Malcolm made no official protest, but understandably it still rankles. Otherwise his victory roll is 'just a few advanced classes; with the sort of horses available and the time to do it in, one was always able to win a few classes, but when it got serious and the

*Colonel Bill Lithgow, Malcolm Wallace's predecessor as* chef d'équipe, *with yet another winning team for Britain,* (left to right) *Richard Meade, Mark Phillips, Stewart Stevens and Mary Gordon-Watson*

chips were down I just did not have the time to put in, like the professionals can, or horses which were quite up to it.

'The King's Troop, and the Army, have always been good to me, but there was just not quite enough time. It's a full-time job. I continued batting on for quite some time, but that same situation went on and I was working on the law of diminishing returns, putting more and more in and getting less and less out. So I decided to call it a day, and switched the emphasis to race-riding, which I could do in an amateur way and enjoy, though I couldn't event in an amateur way and enjoy it.'

He bought a horse from Princess Anne in 1980, took out a permit to train it himself on Salisbury Plain and won three point-to-point races, and a race at Lingfield. 'I then sold him and came to the Troop – I didn't think I had time to do more than be CO and look after the event team, but having done one year I reckon I can, so I've bought one racehorse and put in an order for one more.' He has also applied to the Jockey Club for a permit to train again, at the Troop's headquarters at St John's Wood, London. Not many gallops there, 'but at least I can get him fit up and down the hill.

'The thing about racing is that my ambitions are lower. I can get a thrill out of finishing third in a novice chase, but I would get no thrill out of finishing third in a novice trial. We won the last competition we went in for and I said to Caroline (his wife), "I think we'll call it a day. I didn't particularly enjoy today and we actually had a winner."'

Malcolm Wallace began to act as *chef d'équipe* in 1975, but only of the teams at CCIs – the less important international events – not at championships. He did this for four years until Colonel Bill Lithgow retired, and then there was a short-list of Wallace and fellow Army officer Targik Kopanski to replace him. Wallace was thirty-one years old then, and the Selection Committee decided he was too young, so it went to Kopanski, but only for two years, before he left the Army. 'Then there was only me, so it didn't matter how old I was,' Malcolm recalls with a laugh. Whatever doubts the committee might still have felt were to be swept away over the next few seasons as the British team regained the position it had held in that halcyon period around the Mexico and Munich Olympics.

Far from his youth proving a handicap, it developed

*The ill-fated Loughlin ridden by Penny Moreton in the Mexico Olympics. The horse was later put down after suffering a leg injury*

into a considerable asset, although Major Wallace had a different approach to Colonel Bill Lithgow, who had been something of a father-figure to his squad. 'I think they found it easier to kick around someone of thirty than sixty,' says Wallace, but only jokingly: there was no lessening in discipline, but it was self-imposed discipline of intelligent, adult riders whose aim at a championship is exactly the same as that of their *chef d'équipe* – to win.

'I'm chums with most of them, which by and large is an advantage. Sometimes it can go the other way, but I know them all pretty well, and I can identify with them. I see them quite often off the field of battle, so to speak.'

The winter is very much an 'off' period as far as Malcolm Wallace is concerned, a time when he forgets about eventing and concentrates on hunting, shooting and, his great love, racing, as much as his time allows. 'I deliberately have a total break. People ask me questions around Christmas time like "Have you heard about so-and-so's horse?" and I haven't a clue. When I come back into it all, about Badminton time, I'm fresh, wanting to have a go. The riders are very much the same, they all go off skiing, or to Australia or somewhere. I don't think you can be on the ball the whole year round – unless you're Chris Collins!'

Malcolm Wallace's friendship with Chris Collins, chairman of the Selection Committee, is one of the major touchstones of the team's success these days. The two men have in common a keen interest in racing – Wallace rides out on Collins' horses and sometimes in races too – their London offices are only a mile apart, and they often meet for lunch. They are on the same wavelength and each respects the other's abilities, making them into a formidable backroom team.

'In early spring I phone all the riders, those I haven't seen during the winter, arranging to meet them. And then Peter (Scott-Dunn, the team's official veterinary surgeon) and I have what I call the "Vampire Run". We go around all the horses on the championship short-list at their homes and take blood from them, and send the samples off for analysis. And we put out a medical history sheet which the riders have to fill in. That's the first serious contact we have with the riders about their horses' health, their financial situation and so on.'

Although Malcolm is not on the Selection Committee they, naturally, pay great heed to his advice before making any selections. 'Chris is not a great one for a vote anyway, and by and large in the end the horses tend to select themselves, but before the short-list is chosen my opinion is always asked. I know them all, and if it's temperament, or a horse's soundness or

something like that, it's probably been on a team before and Peter and I will be able to tell the Selectors about it.'

But it is in the lead-up to the championships that Major Malcolm Wallace, *chef d'équipe*, really has to swing into top gear. He does all the administration for the final training sessions: usually these are held at Lord and Lady Hugh Russell's well-equipped Bathampton House, at Wylye, and if, for example, the riders wish to use one of the local racehorse trainer's all-weather gallops, Malcolm makes the arrangements. He makes all the travel arrangements, the boats and planes, trains and horseboxes, in close liaison with Michael Bullen of Pedens; arranges grooms' quarters and bedding; finds out which trainers are coming with which rider and makes arrangements for them. 'I put the thing together, and I must say I get enormous help from Stoneleigh; and I have to arrange all the sponsorships, Lavenham's for the horses' rugs, Simpson's for the team's clothes, Lambourn horseboxes and, for the 1983 European Championships in Frauenfeld, three Range Rovers. All that, even down to ordering the sizes of the girls' skirts!'

Although he does not interfere with the riders' training, he is only too happy to lend a hand where necessary, and a few years ago, feeling that some of them were taking the wrong path in getting their horses fit, asked Fred Winter, the leading National Hunt trainer, if he would help. Mr Winter, who has two daughters who ride in horse trials, 'agreed immediately. He was marvellous, and gave a long and detailed talk about how he got his racehorses fit and ready for racing. I'm sure it helped a tremendous amount.

'Once they get to their destination, I leave them totally be for about three days, and hardly tell them to do anything or be anywhere.

'There's normally a period of extreme tension at that sort of time and it's quite good to let that bubble burst. So I like to get to a competition earlier rather than later, to get the nervous bit out of their systems. The old hands don't mind a bit, but with some of the youngsters we get the odd scene or two – but that all blows over.

'For the dressage days, all I do is to make sure they're in the right place at the right time, in the right kit; and make sure they don't go in with martingales on or anything like that. But they're all pretty professional, I don't have any worries there.'

Once the team is at a championship in good order, the *chef d'équipe*'s job mostly revolves around the cross-country day. For a start, he is responsible for which of the six members of the squad are included in the official team: in championships, though not of course at Olympic Games, each country fields up to six riders, four in the team and two going as individuals. And he has to decide the order of starting. 'Chris is always there, of course, so we discuss the team together. And I always talk to the riders about the order of going, and if possible let them go in the order they prefer. Sometimes it is not possible, then I have to make a decision. Chris's great theory is that we run a form of "open government".'

Wallace's assistant, Eddie Farmer, goes round the cross-country course and the steeplechase course, taking detailed measurements of distances – every second over the time in the chase could cost medal-winning penalties, but there is no point in completing the course half a minute early — and, with graph paper and a measuring stick, draws every fence on the course to scale. These are photocopied, and, two nights before the cross-country day, there is a briefing. Every rider is given a copy of the drawings, and every fence is discussed.

'The idea is that everyone should know all the options. I'm not expert enough to tell them where to jump the fence, but I chair a meeting. Everyone puts in their ideas, and if people go away looking thoughtful I know we've won one battle. I am sure it has won us at least one Championship – the European in Horsens, 1981 – and two CCIs. At Horsens they really understood what they were doing, more than any of the other teams. The riders went away from the meeting saying, "I should have thought of that," and went back and looked at the fences again.'

That is why Malcolm Wallace has the meeting two days before the cross-country, not the evening before as used to happen, to give the riders the chance to see the course again. There was a time when 'with no time to go, riders were hearing brand new things and panicking'.

After briefing the riders, he gathers all the helpers, the parents, wives, husbands, boyfriends who have gone along to support the team, and make their own invaluable contribution.

The 'spotters', each of whom will stand beside a problem fence throughout the day, are given a sheaf of being fed back, via Martin Whiteley, some very valu-

five different-coloured pens: 'Their notes about the way a horse has jumped the fence are collected in lots of five, and every horse is a different colour, so it is easy to see instantly who has done what. They tell which route has been taken, and the number of strides, and their general opinion – which is why I only select a few people and a few fences, otherwise you get a lot of opinions from people you don't want.' Martin Whiteley, Chairman of the Horse Trials Committee, ex-international rider and former chairman of the Selection Committee, is in charge of this group of helpers.

'They also mark which particular horse it was, so if some Bulgar goes in and makes a complete mess of it, and then another rider at that sort of level does the same, I don't necessarily discount the route, but if it's Bruce Davidson or Harry Klugmann who have done so then I take note. So I am

*Lord and Lady Hugh Russell chat to Lucinda Prior-Palmer at Luhmühlen, 1979. Final training sessions before major international events are organised by Major Wallace at their Wylye estate*

able information, and when the riders come into the Box (where they have their ten-minute compulsory break before starting the cross-country) they come to me and I run through the course, fence by fence, ignoring any minor information, sticking to points which are of real value. All the riders, from Richard (Meade) down have said they have found that precise briefing to be absolutely invaluable.

'Every now and again it goes wrong. At Luhmühlen (for the 1982 World Championships) it went wrong with Rachel (Bayliss) – she wanted to go to one side of the water, but it was riding badly, so I persuaded her to go to the left. It was the wrong decision. It was my fault, and certainly her trainer would agree with me! She's too polite to say so, but I'm sure she would too.'

All the time, Chris Collins is with him, with a stop-watch, alarm, calculator and goodness knows what else, working out the scores in his head and scribbling

them on to a piece of paper to give Malcolm the tactical position, 'So that I can say, "You've got to go fast" or "You've got to go slow and get round" or whatever.' And at the same time Ann Scott-Dunn, wife of the vet, is working out the precise position. 'It is very much a team effort, co-ordinated by me, but with major contributions from many others.'

As well as looking after the horses on the course, he must make sure the others, who have completed their day's work, are looked after, and he always has two vehicles and drivers whose sole job it is to ferry the grooms to wherever they need to be.

The whole job is, says Major Malcolm Wallace, 'an absolute natural for a Regimental Officer – the welfare of the grooms, the morale of the riders, the administration, movement, feeding, the whole thing is an officer's bread and butter.' And he has nothing but thanks for the time he has been given off to do it, even though, as CO of the King's Troop, it is less than it used to be: 'Then I only had files to deal with, now it's men and horses. You could stick a file in a tray and leave it for a few days but you can't do that with men and with horses. But because I've got such damned good officers and senior NCOs I can take slightly more time than I would otherwise be able to.'

Much of the method of running the team Malcolm Wallace has inherited, but he makes 'no apology for Americanising the team. The riders now go in a uniform, identical tracksuits, and I'm sure it helps. At Horsens, the first time we really got that act together, the British team came down to the training area, all the riders dressed the same, all the grooms dressed the same, all the horses dressed the same, with hand-stitched leather headcollars with buffed-up brass plates with "Great Britain" written on them, and the German *chef d'équipe* said later, "As soon as we saw you coming we realised you'd won. We looked up and thought, Christ, here come the British." I used not to think like that, but now I'm sure it gives the whole squad a tremendous *esprit de corps*. I think it genuinely does weld them together as a smart, efficient fighting unit.

'I think what one is doing is modernising a sport the British have always been frightfully good at in a frightfully British sort of way. I don't criticise the old methods, goodness knows we won enough gold medals with them, but we are moving with the times.'

How long Malcolm Wallace remains Britain's *chef d'équipe* depends upon his own career, whether or not he stays in the Army: but until the Los Angeles Olympics at least. When he does leave his successor will inherit a squad, and a way of running it, formidable by any standards.

*Before the European Championships at Frauenfeld in 1983 – Malcolm Wallace, Lorna Clarke, Michael Tucker (who later withdrew), Ginny Holgate, Lucinda Green and Diana Clapham*

# 3
# Badminton

The 1983 Badminton Horse Trials will always be remembered for the fact that Lucinda Green, World Champion and three-day-event rider extraordinaire, won the Whitbread Trophy for a record fifth time.

To win Badminton once is considered an achievement, one which eludes a multitude of hopefuls; but to end up in the main arena and be presented with the trophy on five occasions is like something out of a fairytale.

That magnificent performance was just another chapter of success in the history of the actual trials; since they were inaugurated in 1949 there have been many magic moments, and over the years Badminton has been greatly influential in promoting the sport of three-day eventing.

The first Badminton trials, advertised at the time as a 'Horse Event', was won by John Shedden on Golden Willow, and during the next eleven years British riders reigned supreme. Only Captain Hans Schwarzenbach from Switzerland interrupted the flow when he was successful on Vae Victis in 1951. Two years later, when the European Championships were held at this event, he finished third, on the same horse, behind Lawrence Rook, who partnered Starlight XV, and Frank Weldon with Kilbarry.

It is interesting to note that at those 1953 European Championships, the winning British team was the only squad of riders who actually managed to finish the course. But, after a period of complete British domination, foreign riders started to make their presence felt, Bill Roycroft coming over from Australia to win the event in 1960 on Our Solo.

Roycroft blazed the trail for the Australians and it was really no surprise when his countryman, Laurie Morgan, came over with Salad Days and emulated that victory the following year. Twelve months later, however, Britain bounced back when Anneli Drummond-Hay took the honours with the great Merely-a-Monarch.

The official programme for the very first trials in 1949 was an exercise in how things should be done – it left no question unanswered. In those far-off days a shilling was good enough to give you entrance to the Duke of Beaufort's Gloucestershire estate to watch the horse trials. Charabancs came a bit dearer: for a twenty-six seater you would be required to part with the princely sum of £2.10s. It was also an age when the British Horse Society was based at number 66 Sloane Street.

From the very start, Badminton has been a winner, partly because everyone involved believes totally in what they are doing and partly because the trials are staged in such delightful surroundings on the late Duke of Beaufort's beautiful estate. Even those who are not particularly interested in horses go along to have a look, forming part of the quarter of a million visitors who regularly visit Badminton over the four days of the horse trials. Apart from watching quality horses negotiate some thirty-three fences over four and a half miles of cross-country, there are also plenty of other things to do, which include having a picnic, shopping at the many stalls, or merely walking a dog in peaceful surroundings.

But if you are there to watch the dressage, cross-country and final show-jumping phase then you will

Right: *The man who won the first ever Badminton Trials, John Shedden on Golden Willow in 1949*

Below: *Captain Hans Schwarzenbach on Vae Victis, winner of the 1951 Badminton and third in the European Championships held there in 1953*

Above: *Looking pensive – Laurie Morgan on Salad Days, a great combination*
Opposite above: *Major Lawrence Rook on Starlight XV, winners of the European Championships at Badminton, 1953*
Opposite below: *The great Bill Roycroft with the highly talented Our Solo*

not feel let down, no matter who wins: for Badminton, still run, as it always has been, in April, does truly have a unique quality about it. Even the names of the obstacles have a ring all their own: the Bull Pens, Deer Park Ditch, the New Moon, the Quarry, the Lake, Huntsman's Leap and the Elephant Trap.

All are built with great care

make sure that if any fence is damaged, it is repaired at once.

Everything, as far as the Badminton course is concerned, is thought out in minute detail by the trials director, Lieutenant Colonel Frank Weldon, a man who loves the sport and who was formerly a successful rider himself. He won the European Championship in 1955 at Windsor – there was no Badminton that year because of the Championship – and Badminton a year later, both times riding the great Kilbarry. A dedicated and knowledgeable man where three-day eventing is concerned, he always has the interests of the riders and their horses at heart. At Badminton in 1983 he made some forthright observations about course building and how courses have changed over the years:

'When I was riding,' he said, 'the fences were all at maximum height and it was most certainly hard on the horses and sometimes on those who were on top of them. Nowadays though, courses, and in particular Badminton, are built to make riders think more.

'Whenever riders walk Badminton for the first time they think, "My goodness, this is big" and get terribly worried and start telling each other Frank Weldon's had another big course built. Then they go around it for a second time and suddenly realise it is not as bad as they thought. The big danger is when they walk it for a third time and think it all looks rather easy.

'In fact,' he said, smiling, 'that is when they make a big mistake because the first rule is never be over-confident. I know it happens because I have done it myself in the old days.

'But even if the course is big and does worry some of the riders, it must be remembered that there are always plenty of alternatives for them to take, and what it all comes down to is that it is the rider who must make the right decisions. Sometimes when it is a pre-Olympic

*Badminton attracts some two hundred thousand spectators, including the Queen Mother, the Queen and Master – the late Duke of Beaufort, on whose estate the trials are staged*

and expertise by Alan Willis and Gilbert Thornbury. Badminton does not just happen, it takes anything up to six months to prepare everything on the course for those four days in April. When the trials take place Messrs Willis and Thornbury are always on hand to

*Now a show jumper but then an event rider, Anneli Drummond-Hay flying high with Merely-a-Monarch*

*Lucinda Green is the only person in eventing history to have won the Badminton Horse Trials five times – on Be Fair in 1973 (above), Wide Awake in 1976 (above far right), George in 1977 (below left), Killaire in 1979 (below right)* and *Regal Realm in 1983 (above centre)*

year, or when a World or European Championship is coming up in the near future, I have the Badminton course built with that in mind. We take six months to build the course and I do it with the help of two splendid men who are craftsmen. They know exactly what they are doing and what I want.'

He knows what it takes to win a major three-day event, and is adamant that it is not the German way of doing things that is the best. 'The Germans place their emphasis on dressage and shorten their courses. But it should be cross-country that wins events because that is what eventing is all about.'

But eventing at Badminton is not just about the cross-country course, the horses and the riders. In 1983 Weldon realised that there were several funds which needed help; as a result certain obstacles on the course were specifically designed so that they would stand out and the public would notice them. One was for the British Field Sports Society, which was then trying to counter the politically motivated threat to fox-hunting. There was also help for the Grand National Appeal, and the British International Equestrian Fund,

which is used to send our equestrian teams abroad. Weldon made sure that everyone had a look-in and gave them all his whole-hearted support.

Foxhunting was very close to the Duke of Beaufort's heart and even in his eighties, he was still seen riding to hounds. Sadly he died in February 1984. Hunting is part of our national heritage and Weldon and those who have a deep love of the country and field sports do not want to see it destroyed. Perhaps that is considered by some to be politicising but why should those concerned not have the right to fight back and protect a way of life they consider to be part of Great Britain?

One of the reasons this country is so good at producing top-class event riders is the fact that many of them were taught to ride in the hunting field; riding across country, no matter how big the fences, comes naturally because they have been doing it all their lives. What better way is there to learn to judge pace and distance than riding to hounds? When politicians enter the arena and start throwing their weight around, people sometimes have to stand up and be counted and, on occasions, do in fact need a fighting fund.

*Up, up and away – Lucinda Green tackles the Quarry on Beagle Bay, 1983* (right to left)

Some of the essential expenses involved might never occur to the average person. For instance, how do you cope with 200,000 people who might want to go to the loo at the same time? It is an awesome thought, and building portable lavatories costs a great deal of money. Proof that they are needed, desperately on occasions, can be witnessed by the long queues of patient women on cross-country day!

A bonus for riders is that everyone gets free stabling – in contrast to the show-jumping world where at many venues even the most famous riders have to pay for these facilities. There is also forage for the horses, and accommodation and food for the grooms. This highly civilised approach shows that those concerned care about the 'behind the scenes workers' and go out of their way to make sure they are comfortable during their four- or five-day stay.

*Colonel Frank Weldon, the man in charge at Badminton*

As with any successful venture, those most in the public eye – in this instance, Frank Weldon – are backed up by an army of willing helpers, and although the man at the helm steers them in the right direction, it is that army which makes it all possible on the day. That is why the contribution made by car park attendants (who have to cope with thousands of cars), programme sellers, ring officials and a multitude of other people should never be underestimated.

Badminton might only take place once a year but it is now a major institution and, indeed, something of a fairy godmother to the British Horse Society. In the past the Society has received between £80,000 and £90,000 from the Badminton Trials, money which is chanelled into the various aspects of the Society's work.

But running the trials is extremely expensive and to make a success of it the organisers have to be thinking in terms of £300,000.

Even though 200,000 to 250,000 people visit Badminton each year from all parts of the globe, the event would probably not be possible without the tremendous help and financial encouragement from Whitbread, who provide the winner's trophy and cash prizes to the tune of £20,000.

*Behind the scenes, cleaning tack and preparing for the event is as important as riding*

When Mr John Burbidge, chairman of SR Direct Mail, was presented with the Whitbread Trophy by the Queen in 1983, after Lucinda Green had won with Regal Realm, he made a point of going over to the Whitbread tent and thanking the officials of the company for the support they gave Badminton. That was a gesture which went down very well indeed.

Nowadays the winner of Badminton receives a total of £5000. Prize money like this is well and truly welcomed by all riders because it costs a great deal to keep a horse in training and, because of the demanding nature of the sport, event horses, unlike show jumpers, can only be asked to compete in a limited number of three-day events. The runner up at Badminton is presented with a cheque for £3250, the third £2250, the fourth £1500, the fifth £1000, and so on right down to twelfth place. The 1983 winner was also presented with a saddle by the Worshipful Company of Saddlers, and the Whitbread spurs went to the British rider with the best cross-country score, who was under twenty-five and not entitled to wear the adult Union Jack badge, with £250 also going to the owner of the horse.

Added to those prizes were a multitude of other awards: a Silver Jubilee Challenge Plate presented by Miss Flavia Phillips, which went to the most successful rider on his, or her, own horse, plus £75 to the owners of every horse which finished the competition; £30 to the groom of each horse that finished, and a special prize of a bronze head trophy and a rosette presented by the National Light Horse Improvement Society, to the owner of the most successful horse sired by an HIS Premium stallion, provided it finished in the first twelve places. All these prizes, thoughtfully provided, mean so much to everyone who takes part in eventing, and the fact that most of those connected with the horse are remembered proves that the sport is rather special.

At Badminton the welfare of the horses comes first: there is always a team of seven veterinary surgeons available to give the best possible treatment if it is required. Delay is cut to a minimum because at every fence there are trained people with radio contact to a central base, and the moment something untoward happens to rider, or horse, the news can be flashed back to headquarters in seconds. The whole operation is run with military precision, which is why it all works to perfection. Without this direct contact too many things could go wrong; but at Badminton that is not allowed to happen, which is why it is such a successful event and will go on being so for many years to come.

A special mention must be made of the Duke of Beaufort, on whose land the trials are staged. The rolling acres of old turf, which more often than not make the going perfect for jumping, are used wisely and with care, each fence on the course being cleverly situated to use the land to the best effect. When, in 1983, a tree fell down, Frank Weldon was quick to take advantage of the windfall and used it as one of the obstacles: nothing, not even dead trees, is wasted.

Watching over all, in stately fashion, is the Duke's beautiful house, once painted by Canaletto. It is a part of old England which will, one hopes, be with us for all time.

*Weldon makes use of everything, including fallen trees. John Tulloch on Bower Grit at the aptly named Windfall obstacle*

It is in Badminton House that Her Majesty The Queen, Prince Philip and most of the Royal family stay when they attend the trials. From the house they are able to look right across the lush green acres and see the Lake which, for the public, is one of the most popular obstacles on the cross-country course. It was here that Captain Mark Phillips, the only man, to date, to have won Badminton four times, took a tremendous ducking in the water when his horse fell. Eventually Captain Phillips ended up on the bank, with his legs in the air, water pouring like a waterfall from his riding boots! Press photographers had a field-day, and that particular picture was used in equestrian and non-equestrian magazines and newspapers around the world. It was another classic example of how easily Badminton makes news and, in doing so, automatically promotes itself.

The press, too, are not backward in seeing the value of a venue like Badminton. They know from past experience that there will always be a story there: all they have to do is wait long enough for it to break. It might be the size of the fences, the number of entries, or the Queen buying a pair of gloves at one of the stalls. There is always something, and that is why reporters and photographers continue to turn up in their hundreds, in the hope of that exclusive picture or story that will make their journey worthwhile. So far, not many have returned home disappointed.

*You can take a horse to water, but you can't always make him jump. Captain Mark Phillips on Brazil in a case of going . . . going . . . gone! But all ended without injury, although a soaking was in order, at Badminton in 1976. The photographers had a field day!*

*Mark Phillips, the only man to have won
Badminton four times. It started with
Great Ovation in 1971 (above left) and
1972 (above right), followed by the
Queen's horse Columbus in 1974 (below
left) and Lincoln in 1981 (below right)*

The man in charge of the press at Badminton is Jim Gilmore, himself a writer and, therefore, a man who knows what the majority of the press corps requires.

*Man of the media – Jim Gilmore, the press officer at Badminton*

His is the unenviable task of issuing photographers' passes to the main ring for the show-jumping phase. It is, of course, after this that the Queen presents the Whitbread trophy to the winner, and there is always much juggling for position on the part of the picture takers to get the best possible shot. But Mr Gilmore copes admirably with it all and each year most, if not quite all, go away happy.

Perhaps the most interesting point from the press side is that newspapers which do not normally go out of their way to cover eventing, almost certainly send someone to Badminton. Over the years the trials have attracted many journalists from home and abroad, and each season the numbers seem to increase.

As far as the actual competitors are concerned, their briefing usually takes place place on the Wednesday, when there is also an inspection of the course and, later, an examination of the horses. This takes place at the north front of Badminton House. On Thursday the first section of the dressage is staged, with a showing of the Whitbread films in the evening at the village hall.

Then, on the Friday, the second section of the dressage is run, while Saturday sees the start of the speed and endurance. Anyone who is fit enough goes on to the Badminton horse trials dance in the evening. On Sunday there is the official vetting of the horses, a service in Badminton village church, and in the afternoon the show jumping.

# 4
# Encouraging the Young

For any sport to survive it must encourage its young people, and in this respect eventing is no different from any other activity. If there was no one to take the place of the present-day champions when they retire the whole structure of the sport would fall to pieces. In Britain, fortunately, that is unlikely to happen, since horse trials are run by people who do care and are well aware of the situation. That is why everyone, right up to the top level, goes out of their way to offer advice and assistance to the younger generation of riders. And the youngsters in their turn are not slow to accept help from those who have been very good riders themselves in the past, or have spent a lifetime working with competition horses. It would be foolish to ignore their preferred help, and they know it.

Of course, it is not enough just to give the youngsters a pat on the head. What is needed is constructive and, in many cases, financial help. Because of the vast costs involved, many youngsters never break through to the top echelon of the sport; they are only too well aware that, if they did, they would immediately need financial assistance. This is not to say that everything should be made easy for them – it should not. Anyone who has reached the top flight has done so because of a burning desire to succeed, and through a lot of hard work and self-sacrifice. Nobody becomes a champion without a lot of dedication and the will to succeed. Money is important, but it is only one of the ingredients for success – without the others it is useless.

Parents of young hopefuls play their part by offering not only financial assistance but also help and encourage-ment. It can be guaranteed that all the riders in Britain who have made names for themselves in eventing have done so because they had valuable help from their families. Nobody can go it alone; those who think they can are deluding themselves. The huge costs involved can, however, be crippling and that is why, unless a person is very well off, the first thing they look for is a sponsor who, by putting up anything from £1000 to £100,000, can at once ease that burden, or eradicate it.

But it is a double-edged sword, because many companies will not consider sponsorship unless the person receiving the money is a big name and can attract publicity. As explained in the chapter Vital Support, it is very difficult indeed for a virtual unknown to gain massive financial support for several years. First they have to prove their worth, then the companies might be interested. Even then it is still very difficult because eventing, unlike show jumping, does not (at the time of writing) allow prefixes to be added to horses' names, so the only publicity sponsors get is to have their names in the programmes, flashed up occasionally on television, written about in newspapers and magazines, and sometimes mentioned on radio.

But even that is a bit of a hit and miss affair, because although all equestrian journalists go out of their way to mention sponsors, it does depend to a great extent on the amount of space they have at their disposal. It is irksome to be told by a sponsor, as has happened in the past, that if their company's name is not mentioned, they might not find it worthwhile to carry on. That is understandable, but unfortunately all too often journalists have no control over how much of their copy will actually appear in print. There is always a great pressure on space.

On the other hand, some journalists have been instrumental in obtaining sponsorship for riders, by writing stories about them and informing the public about their plight. Without such publicity many sponsorships might never have happened. Those who do plough thousands of pounds' worth of sponsorship into eventing, however, have done and are doing a first-class job.

One of the companies which gives a good deal of help to the youngsters is Range Rover, who pulled off a coup a few years ago by sponsoring Captain Mark Phillips. That was one of the best moves ever made by a sponsor in eventing, but, when the deal was announced, it was also revealed that, at the instigation of Mark Phillips himself, Range Rover was also introducing a bursary scheme for youngsters so that they, too, would

*A great rider who is also concerned about the young ones – Mark Phillips and admirers, maybe future event competitors*

benefit. It was typical of Mark Phillips that in acquiring a very worthwhile sponsorship himself, he should ensure that youngsters would also be helped, receiving training from him, personally, at his home in Gatcombe Park.

The bursary scheme was introduced in 1979 and concentrates on young riders between nineteen and twenty-one. A token of £125 is also awarded, at the discretion of the chairman of the Young Riders' Selection Committee, to a young rider competing in the advanced or open intermediate classes at certain horse trials. In 1983 they were Braintree, Denbigh, Tidworth, Wynyard Park, Sherborne Castle, Locko Park, Claughton, Castle Ashby, Rudding Park and Rotherfield. The money is paid to the British Horse Society, who gives it to whoever is chosen, on submission of trainers' bills. In this way the young person concerned cannot lose his, or her, amateur status.

This is all-important, because if an amateur accepted payment of any kind they would automatically be deemed to have taken professional status, which would destroy any hopes of competing in the Olympic Games. But, as the money is paid to the British Horse Society, no rules are broken and the International Olympic Committee is quite happy about the arrangement. In order to safeguard those concerned, all these things were carefully considered before the scheme was implemented.

Later, in 1981, the Range Rover team set up the annual Young Rider Scholarship under the auspices of the BHS. This award, which is valued at £1500, enables a rider to benefit from tuition in order to prepare for major events, and assists with competition expenses. The first person to win this award was Duncan Douglas, and the second Ginny Strawson, who took the honours in successive years, 1982 and 1983.

In 1981 Ginny Strawson had won the JOIT at Brigstock on Sparrow Hawk and the intermediate on Greek Herb; Belton Park and Wynyard Park novice on Minsmore; the junior final trial at Heckfield on Greek Herb; a team silver medal on the same horse in the Junior European Championships in France, and the Junior at Murton on Minsmore.

After winning the 1982 award, she went to West Germany for a six-week training course with Karl Schultz. She was in incredible form and went from strength to strength all season, crowning her success with a win at the Boekelo International Horse Trials in Holland on Sparrow Hawk II. That event included, Ginny was placed in a total of twenty-three classes during 1982, had twelve outright victories, won the individual gold medal in the Junior European Championships and also won a team silver medal.

*Ginny Strawson and the big-jumping Minsmore at Fontainebleau in 1982*

It was no surprise to see her winning the Range Rover Scholarship – it was well deserved. The presentation took place at the Olympia International Show Jumping Championships in December of that year and was, fittingly, made by Captain Mark Phillips and Mr Jack Reardon, Sales and Marketing Director of Land-Rover Ltd.

Talking about the Range Rover support of eventing, and the young rider category in particular, Ginny said at that time, 'The Award has been invaluable to me, enabling me to get extra tuition and advice. I have been able to strengthen the show-jumping element of my performance. I also think it is most important to have the opportunity of using trainers from other countries to learn from their various methods of training. Thanks to the generosity and encouragement of Range Rover, I

feel I have made great progress and enjoyed my best ever season.

'I was fortunate enough to be invited to attend the training courses at Gatcombe Park. The practical help and advice given by Captain Mark Phillips has been of lasting benefit. I can only say that all the young riders, like myself, who have been fortunate enough to receive practical help from Range Rover, are extremely grateful for their interest and support.'

Another talented young rider is Karen Straker, who rode tremendously well at Badminton in 1983 on Running Bear, after winning the Young Riders' at Brigstock on the same horse. At Badminton she was lying twelfth after the cross-country and although 17.75 penalties in the show jumping dropped her down three places in the final list, it was a fine performance.

If anyone was born to ride horses it was Karen. Her mother, Elaine, was herself a successful competitor, and Karen also has two brothers who compete. One of her finest moments came at Rotherfield Park in 1982 when

*Polly Schwerdt, with Dylan, on her way to a team gold medal in the European Young Riders' Championships at Burghley, 1983*

she won the individual Junior European Championship with Running Bear, and also a team gold. In 1983 she and Running Bear finished second in the European Young Riders' Championships at Burghley and would have won if they had not hit two show-jumping fences. They helped the team to take the gold medal. She was also a member of the winning team at Kalmthout, in Belgium, in 1979.

After she had won the title at Rotherfield, the British Equestrian Writers Association voted her young personality of the year, and presented her with the Vivian Batchelor Trophy. It was a great achievement and crowned a fine year for Miss Straker.

Being blessed with several very, very good young riders is a bonus for any country, and apart from Ginny Strawson and Karen Straker, Britain has riders like Maureen Piggott, elder daughter of the great jockey, Lester. In 1981 Maureen won a team gold medal on Asian Princess in the European Young Riders' Championships at Achselschwang in West Germany, and a year later won a team silver on Hong Kong Discoverer at Fontainebleau. In both she gave highly creditable performances.

Her first horse, however, was Barney II, formerly with Janet Hodgson. He was tried as a four-year-old, bought for Maureen, and then spent his time with Alison Oliver, who had helped Princess Anne in her early riding days. Maureen was to have ridden Barney in the 1979 Junior Championships, but when the horse went lame she had to withdraw.

*Ever onward, Karen Straker and Running Bear at the Junior European Championships, Rotherfield, 1982*

*Like father, like daughter. Maureen Piggott weighing in after competing. Legendary father Lester and mother Susan follow Maureen's progress with pride*

Two years later Cathay Pacific Airways announced that they were sponsoring Maureen. Shortly afterwards Barney's name was changed to Hong Kong Flyer. As a result he very nearly missed coming under orders at Badminton because there was an objection about his name not being registered in time. And so it was decided to keep the name Barney for Badminton. Alas, the story was not to have a fairytale ending because Barney fell, though Maureen did remount and finished the course. Barney did not compete in a three-day

*It looks so easy – Fiona Moore in harmony with Drakenburg*

event after that and subsequently contracted a fatal illness, dying at the age of nine. It must have been a tremendous blow for Maureen. She has since ridden Hong Kong Discoverer at Badminton in 1982 and 1983 but, in the latter, retired during phase D. Maureen was featured in the book by Genevieve Murphy, the *Observer*'s Equestrian Correspondent, *Three Day Eventing, The Badminton Horse Trials*, published during the spring of 1983.

Another young lady with a bright future is Fiona Moore who rides both eventing and show jumping and did very well at indoor shows during 1982. She also attended the Iris Kellett/John Hall course at the Catherston Stud, home of ace dressage rider Jennie Loriston-Clarke.

Fiona is one of the lucky ones to receive help from

the Horse Trials Support Group, and by finishing tenth at Badminton in 1983 on Squire's Holt, she most certainly earned that help. She started with a dressage score of 51.80 penalty points, had 33.60 penalty points across country (which included 13.60 time faults) and just 5.00 in the show-jumping ring, to make a grand total of 90.40. It was a tremendous effort and one which earned her a place on the short-list for the European Championships in Frauenfeld.

Fiona had her first taste of Badminton in the April of 1977, and did well that year to finish eighth on Drakenburg. In 1981 she won the major Boekelo International

*Young and talented, Jonquil Sainsbury on Mr Moon at Gatcombe Park, 1983*

on Squire's Holt, the horse on whom she finished fourth at Burghley a year later. Her other major ride is Kilgowan Lad.

If gold medals were awarded for bravery, then Lucinda Moir, from Closworth, near Yeovil in Somerset, would have a pocketful. This highly talented rider, another who receives financial encouragement from the Horse Trials Support Group, suffered a bad injury eventing, which left her walking with the aid of sticks in 1982. But she recovered from that fall, fought her way back to fitness and was soon back in the saddle. That is the

sort of courage every rider must have to reach the top, because eventing, like National Hunt racing, can be extremely hazardous. All riders, by the law of averages, will come down at some time or another, and must be able to take the rough with the smooth.

Three-day eventing, however, is not just about riding talent and the ability to climb back after falling. There are many young riders who have to struggle very hard indeed just to compete, coping with a job at the same time. One such lady is Fiona Rutherford, who rides a horse called The Editor and who for part of the year works in an office near her home in Surrey. When she is not there, she is working at the Burghley Horse Trials office so she is one of those who is really close to the sport. She may not yet have been selected for championships of any sort, but she, and others like her, are the backbone of eventing and deserve, for sheer effort, to achieve their ambitions. Being good, or successful, at sport is never merely a question of having suitable funds available. As any rider will tell you, it is mostly a question of needing so badly to do something, and then having the stamina to take the knocks and disappointments that go hand in hand with eventing.

It is particularly difficult for someone with just one horse because an eventer can only cope with so many competitions in a season and, therefore, the opportunities are limited. And, of course, if the horse injures himself

in any way both his and his rider's hopes can be completely dashed. For a rider to cope with a job and keep him or herself and the horse in training, calls for a lot of sacrifices. Some people can make them, others just cannot.

Nicola May, daughter of former England cricket captain Peter May, is another young lady destined for the top. Nicola, who lives in Surrey, won the individual Junior European Championship at Punchestown in 1979 on Commodore IV, also taking a team silver. Then, only a year later, she won a team gold at Achselschwang. In 1982 she was runner-up at Bramham on Penny Thorn.

Nicola's mother is Virginia Gilligan, herself a former three-day-event rider. And this is where parents of all young hopefuls must have a special mention, for all the hard work and thought and money that goes to making an event rider. The public sees only brave young people

*A great victory – Karen Straker (Running Bear), Polly Schwerdt (Dylan II), Camilla Murdoch (Rugan) and Ginny Strawson (Minsmore) after winning the European Young Riders' Championships at Burghley, 1983*

riding at horse trials; what they miss is the vast amount of organisation that goes into getting the youngsters there in the first place. The vast amount of miles covered travelling from one place to another in Britain; or arranging flights or boat tickets in order to reach another country to compete – these are no easy matters and the responsibility does, invariably, fall upon the parents. That is why it is vital for any youngster to have full help and encouragement from both mother and father; if it is not forthcoming that girl or boy sets out with such a severe disadvantage that the chances are he or she will be buried under a welter of problems. In all equestrian sports, team work, both in and out of the saddle, is vital for all concerned.

There are occasions, of course, if someone is chosen to represent their country, when a lot of the planning, particularly where the horses are concerned, is, to a certain extent, taken care of on behalf of the competitors. But there will always be those hidden, niggly problems which only willing parents, or the young people themselves, can solve. So for those riders who have to do everything themselves, the troubles mount up, and instead of being relaxed before an event, they may find themselves undergoing much unwanted pressure.

The other advantage of family involvement is that if a rider is doing everything on a very small budget, and has to go to work after riding exercise in the morning, it is comforting to know that someone is going to be around to muck out, groom, feed, or just see that the horse is fine in every way.

Parents are, of course, unpaid help: they are particularly good at writing letters to show secretaries, filling in forms and arranging overnight accommodation. They are useful, too, for running across country delivering messages to their offspring about how to jump a certain fence – and are most essential when it comes to acting as a rug rack before and after a competition!

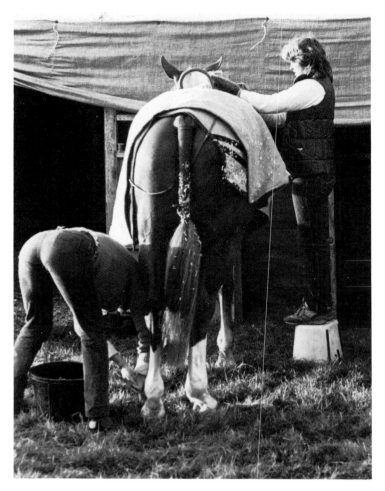

*It's not all riding – Suzanne and Nicola May working hard at Burghley in 1983*

When it comes down to practicalities and reality, family participation is what makes eventing such a great sport: if youngsters want to do well then they have got to have willing parents.

# 5
# The Money Men

Since its inception British Equestrian Promotions, with its head office at 35 Belgrave Square in London, has had one main aim on its agenda – to bring in as much sponsorship to equestrian sports as possible. The company is run by Bob Dean, its chairman, and managing director Raymond Brooks-Ward. In show jumping alone prize

*Raymond Brooks-Ward, Managing Director of British Equestrian Promotions*

money has hit the million-pound mark and eventing, too, has benefited handsomely. Not by as much, but in a very short space of time Hugh Thomas, who also works at BEP, has helped to acquire thousands of pounds' worth of sponsorship. It is an operation which has the good of equestrian sport at heart, but which has come in for a certain amount of criticism in the past.

The people concerned, however, care deeply about equestrian sports and do not mind valid criticism. 'That is all right,' said Brooks-Ward, 'but there have been times when it has been unfair and I certainly do not like that, not so much for myself but for my family, when the muck is flying about in the press. You just have to be big enough to get over it because if you are in the public eye, in any company, you are going to get stick. That I do not mind – what I do not like is inference and innuendo.'

There have been suggestions that British Equestrian Promotions is a monopoly, a charge that Brooks-Ward adamantly refutes and qualifies. 'It is only a monopoly at the horse shows that we administer. We are here to protect the sports' interests but we do not shut the door on other agencies.

'There is nothing to stop anyone else starting up and I certainly would not want to stop them.'

*Would they get any co-operation?*
'Yes, they would, providing they were operating within the guidelines of the sports and not starting a show-jumping or eventing circus. That would be bad for sport.'

*What has BEP done for eventing?*

'When the Midland Bank gave notice that they were withdrawing most of their eventing sponsorship, we were sent for and told to find £320,000, which was quite a tall order. But, it was very fortunate for us that Hugh Thomas came to us – out of the blue – and said he would like to help. He has been a great asset to BEP, knows the sport inside out and has worked very hard to bring in sponsors.

'The criticism we have had about money coming in is the same as in many other sports and that is if a company does not want to go to a certain place in the country, we cannot make them.

'We have almost got back the money we lost from the Midland Bank sponsorship, but it has not gone to every show in the country. Inevitably, some of the smaller events have complained, and we know they have problems and we intend to help. In an ideal world we would try and get every show sponsored, and we have not done too badly because we have got two-thirds covered already.'

*Does BEP take too much out of sponsorship?*

'In some instances in the past, and it may have been wrong, we have taken nothing as far as riders' sponsorship is concerned. We did not take anything because we believe it is a service to the sport.

'From normal sponsorship we would take 12½ per cent, as opposed to other agencies who take between 20 and 25 per cent. We have to have 12½ per cent because of our overheads.'

*So you have never deducted as much as 40 per cent?*

'Absolutely not – never. We also only draw a straight fee from the shows we run.'

At the end of each financial year the profits are divided – 30 per cent goes to the British Horse Society, 30 per cent to the British Show Jumping Association, 30 per cent to Brooks-Ward and 10 per cent to British Equestrian Promotions.

That is certainly not overcharging when one considers how hard everyone at BEP works to make the whole sponsorship structure viable for all concerned. The point is that if there were several agencies involved, the equestrian authorities would have a much greater problem making sure everything was running smoothly and that the integrity of the sport was being upheld.

Neither Brooks-Ward, nor anyone else working at BEP, has ever made any secret of the money that is channelled into sponsorship, or where it eventually goes. There have been people, however, who want to read something that is just not there either into the way he behaves, or how his company operates.

*How did the company come into operation?*

'Bob Dean, who had been looking after sponsorship since 1950,' says Brooks-Ward, 'decided that it was no good being a one-man band. I was with Odhams and Gunn in Dover Street at the time and Bob asked me if I would like to join him. I had known him since 1950. Well, I thought about it, talked with my partner, and decided to accept the offer. When I started with BEP my contribution was about £20,000 worth of accounts in those days. So, the company was started up as a separate entity from the British Horse Society and Show Jumping Association so that it would have more versatility and be self-governing, with a board of directors. I wanted the incentive to do it and I did not want to be an officer of the BHS or BSJA, for obvious reasons. In my view, I do not think in a commercial, competitive world you can run that sort of thing within an organisation. It has to be separate.

'The decision was made, and to date it has proved to be the right one. We have made mistakes, of course, everyone has, but we do not make too many since all of the people here know the sports involved. As such, we are highly unlikely to go against any doctrine laid down by the equestrian disciplines.

'Most of our sponsorship comes from inquiries to us from companies all over the country. What we do is service the grass roots of equestrian sport as well as the major things – in other words, work from the base of the pyramid up. I would think now that the amount of money in equestrian sponsorship is about a million pounds.'

It really is remarkable that show jumping, dressage and eventing have so much prize money being injected into them every year. But the big question is, if Bob Dean and Brooks-Ward had not started BEP, would as much money be servicing the sports? It must be considered doubtful, if only on the assumption that, were a dozen or so agencies involved, each would have to take out a percentage of the cash they pulled in for sponsorship. This, obviously, would mean less money for the sports involved. It could, however, also be argued that more agencies would encourage more money, but as that does not always work.

What is certain is that everything is brilliantly co-ordinated at the moment and, as far as records show, there is no dissent among those who are the recipients of a percentage of the profits at Stoneleigh – headquarters of both the BHS and BSJA.

Whenever hard times come it is usual for official complaints to be voiced over the way things are being run. So far – although there have been outside complaints – the backing, has been solidly *for* British Equestrian Promotions.

And, when you talk to Brooks-Ward at length, you discover that even his ambitions are tied up with work and the long-term projects in hand.

'My ambition,' he says, 'is to make sure that the whole of equestrian sport is on a firm basis of sponsorship at all levels. I would also like to make sure that all our amateur riders in eventing, show jumping and dressage are amply covered with sponsorship.'

That is a tall order, but one which he is aiming to achieve because he knows how important it all is to the future of horse sports and the people in them. But reaching the top in his given field has not been easy, as he willingly relates:

'When I was on the show circuit and my wife was at home looking after the boys, when I returned she used to say to them, "This is your father".'

That just highlights the fact that reaching the top can be hard, and that many pleasures, such as being at home with one's family, have to be sacrificed because there is just not enough time in the day to fit everything in.

'But I am lucky,' said Brooks-Ward, 'in having a wife like Dinnie who is totally loyal and helpful to me and my career.'

For relaxation, Brooks-Ward hunts once a week and is Joint-Master of the Enfield Chase, something of which he is proud.

'I have hunted for twenty-seven seasons,' he says, 'beagles, bassets and foxhounds. If I did not do that I would go mad. It is only one day a week now, but it is enough to keep me sane. I usually get up at 6.00 a.m., muck out the horses, which, incidentally, we keep at home, and then I make my way to the office, eventually returning home at 8.00 p.m. And, really, hunting does not cost me any more than being a member of a good golf club. I also love sailing and we keep a boat.'

*Who does he think has had the biggest impact on eventing in recent years?*

'You cannot quantify what Princess Anne has done for equestrian sport. It is, I suppose, one of the major contributions in the last twenty years and there are two reasons. First of all here was the Queen's daughter proving that she had the guts, tenacity and ability to ride and train and fit everything in to a very busy schedule.

'Secondly, her mother did not go out and pay £80,000 or so for a horse. When Princess Anne won the European

Three-Day Event Championship it was on Doublet – a horse the Queen bred at home. In fact, it was going to be Prince Philip's polo pony at one time. And Goodwill, another of her mounts, was a former show jumper. Princess Anne is also very generous in her praise of others and means it. She is very generous giving credit elsewhere.'

*Who does he admire most in eventing?*

'In all sports you have to have stars and one of the reasons eventing is on top is because of Lucinda Green. She is brilliant and to win Badminton five times and on different horses is incredible.'

Apart from Bob Dean and Brooks-Ward there are also several other people who work at BEP and each has a vital role to play. They are experts in their chosen fields and the company owes them all a great deal.

*What are the qualities he sees in Hugh Thomas?*

'He is somebody who knows the sport as a competitor, course builder and as an organiser – so the vital elements are there. Secondly, I knew he was a good businessman. It is no good having somebody who knows the sport but knows nothing about business. Hugh is also a very good public speaker.'

*When the Midland Bank stopped its major sponsorship, Hugh Thomas (here with Martin Whiteley) was given the job of finding more money for eventing*

John Stevens has also made a great contribution to equestrian sports and Brooks-Ward is quick to praise him.

'John is one of the most experienced men we have,' he says, 'a sort of elder statesman and a person on whom

*Thinking ahead – Neil Fairley of British Equestrian Promotions*

*Man of experience – John Stevens after walking the course at Burghley, 1983*

we all rely a great deal. If we are not certain about something we always check with him because the chances are he will know the answer. He is also a perfect gentleman.'

*What of Bob Dean?*
'Without him none of this would have been possible. He is a great man and totally dedicated. Show jumping and eventing owe him a great deal – and so do I.'

Another man making his mark at BEP is Neil Fairley. 'He is number two in the company to me,' says Brooks-

Ward, 'and is responsible for other sponsorship, apart from eventing. We are always open with people and give them the option of sponsoring show jumping, eventing or dressage. They tell us what suits them.

'Neil was a captain in the King's Troop and I watched him at work there and thought he was the right sort of bloke for me. He is keen, bright, went to Durham University, and Staff College. I had my eyes on him for about six months before grabbing him after he left the King's Troop.'

So, with sponsorship in equestrian sport on the one million pound mark, Bob Dean and Brooks-Ward are rightly proud that they have played starring roles in the success story. But no matter how much more money British Equestrian Promotions pull in for the good of all, the chances are there will still be those who will complain and suggest, perhaps, that they should have a part of the action.

# 6
# Burghley

Each autumn people flock to the Burghley Horse Trials, in Lincolnshire, attracted by the prospect of seeing top-class eventing. The event's success is made possible by a most remarkable man, Charles Stratton, who possesses those rare qualities, good manners, and the ability to get on with practically everyone he meets. He has

*Charles Stratton, the Director of Burghley*

overcome major heart by-pass operations with great courage and now talks about his work with tremendous enthusiasm.

In the final analysis, it is thanks to Charles Stratton that Burghley is the success it is today. The course is always one of the best, and the facilities and organisation are second to none.

'I have been involved with the horse world for a long time,' Stratton says, 'and since 1953 have been a steward at Wembley. And my aim, having decided to work with and for those in equestrian sport, was to try and reach the top and put on a really good show. In 1972 we tried to get something going at Syon Park, but that fell by the wayside, and I started commentating and writing. But always, in the back of my mind, I wanted to run a very good show.

'Well, at the end of 1977 I was offered Burghley at the same time as preparing to organise a show at Milton Keynes. I decided to take Burghley, something I had always been involved in. James Grose had done the spade work and now I could carry on and make it bigger and better. The goal was always there to get to the organisational top and yet make it good for the public. That was on the top of my list.'

That Stratton has achieved his goal, there is no doubt and, with Remy Martin now putting in such massive financial backing, the event is sure to continue to be a winner. When Remy Martin decided to plough money into Burghley and several one-day meetings, it was one of the best things that could have happened to the sport. It was also a just reward for Stratton to be given such tremendous backing after all the hard work and effort he has put into the Lincolnshire project.

'TI had sponsored us before,' he says, 'and were very good. But I had agreed with Lord Exeter before he died that we should up the money. That did not work out, and so I asked Hugh Thomas of British Equestrian Promotions to find us something.'

The new sponsorship was announced at the end of 1982 and in 1983 Remy Martin had its first Burghley Horse Trials. The company agreed to put in a quarter of a million pounds over a three-year period.

'If one did not have a sponsor to this value,' says Stratton, 'we would have to charge £50 for membership, and nobody, least of all me, wants to do that. The

*The man everyone admired – the late Marquess of Exeter at Burghley in 1974*

*Bird's-eye view of Lucinda Green and Shannagh, between roads and tracks and cross-country*

*How to take the Open Ditch Palisade – triple Olympic gold medallist Richard Meade on Kilcashel in 1983*

*Sweat, style and courage – Jim Wofford riding Carawich at Burghley in 1983*

present situation allows us to keep the costs of membership down to £20, for which the individual gets into the car park and has a member's badge and a guest badge, among other things. It all works very well, but we are only able to do it because of a big sponsorship.'

He also points out, rightly, that Burghley plays its part in helping the equestrian world as a whole, because any surplus cash made there is automatically channelled back to the British Horse Society. 'In 1982,' says Stratton, 'we sent the BHS a cheque for £49,300, and the year before that one for £51,200.'

Together with the money that Badminton also sends to the British Horse Society, the future of the horse in sport is guaranteed. As always, it is planning and organisation that makes everything work so well, which is why, as soon as one Burghley meeting is over, another is already being planned by Stratton. 'Directly it is finished, I am thinking of the next year's event,' he says. 'I have one woman permanently employed on accounts and trade stands, and from October to May I do two days a week. From 1 May my secretary comes to work full time and I have a permanent summer staff of four in all. It all goes very well and the people I have up here are tremendous and, like me, believe totally in what we are doing. No one person can do everything and I am very fortunate in having very good staff.'

In the late seventies, however, Stratton's dreams and ambitions were almost destroyed when he was informed that he was very ill and had just three months to live.

'In fact, my wife Anne was told I was a mental case and beyond hope, and that was why I decided to seek the best advice in London, and have a series of tests. It

*Lady Victoria Leatham, the President of Burghley, presenting a trophy to Mary Hunter on Bugsy Malone*

was then discovered I needed open-heart surgery and eventually I had two by-passes put in. Anne was far more worried than me but, thank goodness, everything turned out all right. I must say, at this stage, how good the British Horse Society was to me during and after my illness. The people there always stood by me, and I will never be able to thank them enough for what they did.'

But no man, no matter how brave he is, can carry the burden of illness and cope with the running of a major event like Burghley, particularly when they have just stepped into the job, as Stratton had when he discovered he had a heart problem. That is why he is pleased and proud to thank his wife and give her a lot of credit for his success.

'I relied tremendously on Anne and still do. She knows as much about the job as I do, and we went into it together. She is very much a part of it. While Burghley is on we become extremely busy and Anne is always there to look after the guests, and make sure that everything goes smoothly for them. One always relies tremendously on one's wife.

'We both thoroughly enjoy what we do and when Lord Exeter was alive he was always tremendously enthusiastic, keen about the event, and when I first came to Burghley he gave me every encouragement. And I am very pleased now that Lady Victoria Leatham is president of Burghley.'

*Bill Thomson, a great course designer and official Clerk of the Course at Burghley*

When Stratton talks about the Burghley Horse Trials, which take place in 600 acres of beautiful countryside, it is obvious that he is a man passionately involved with the sport of eventing. He also cares about the horses and riders who compete there, as do all the staff and, in particular, Bill Thomson, a great course designer. He has a wealth of experience and, before any event at Burghley, is always prepared to discuss the course and his reasons for designing it the way he did. Bill is, in fact, the official Clerk of the Course.

*In the swim together, Italian Alessandro Argenton on – or rather nearly off – Albino II at Burghley in 1971*

*Overleaf: David Merret and Queen's Poet highlight the beauty of Burghley House*

*Calling a taxi? No, just negotiating the Lower Trout Hatchery at Burghley. Jemima Johnson on Timber Knight*

*Without them it wouldn't happen – course builders Anthony Ffooks and Philip Herbert, who prepare and look after the course at Burghley*

'My knowledge of event courses is, naturally, limited,' Charles Stratton says, 'but before we look at the course each year we have a talk and Bill always places the emphasis on safety. There is no point in killing horses, and when a horse gets hurt the spectators, rightly, get fed up, because that is not what eventing is all about.

'The courses at Burghley are built within the stipulated heights and spreads and if riders think they are a bit big, we have put in alternatives to deal with that. That way, they do not have to jump anything they do not want to and, in any case, the course is inspected by the technical delegate. Also, helping Bill are assistant Clerks of the

Course Philip Herbert and Anthony Ffooks. When Bill finally retires, he will be sorely missed. He has been very valuable to us over the years, and he is a great chap.'

All connected with Burghley know that if the fences on the cross-country course are too big, and horses get hurt, there will be a public outcry. But that is not the reason the obstacles are always fairly built: the organisers' own sense of fair play would not allow them to take unnecessary chances and the horses' welfare is always uppermost in their minds.

When Lord Exeter died some people thought that might be the end of Burghley, but that was most certainly not the case. As Stratton points out: 'The Trustees have told me that Burghley will go on from now until the foreseeable future, and my next objective is to try and get the 1986 World three-day-event Championship; but I do know that the Australians have applied for it.'

What does a man like Stratton, who appears to be one of the few people who knows what he wants to do in life, like most about running Burghley? 'We love to welcome overseas riders,' he says, 'but the most pleasure I get is seeing a British win, and hearing our national anthem played. That is what really pleases me.'

In 1962 Captain James Templer won the individual European title on M'Lord Connolly, beating the Russian Gazyumov on Granj, with Jane Wykeham-Musgrave back in third place on Ryebrooks. Although a Briton had taken the individual honours, it was Russia who produced the team winners. They beat Ireland, with Britain back in third place.

Four years later Burghley staged the World Championships for the first time and it was the Argentinian, Captain Carlos Moratorio, who won the individual on Chalan. Richard Meade finished second on Barberry, with Virginia Freeman-Jackson, of Ireland, back in third place on Sam Weller. Only two teams finished that year, victory going to Ireland, with Argentina in the runner-up position.

In 1974 the World title returned to Burghley and helped make a little bit of equestrian history, because it was then that Bruce Davidson won the first of his two World Championships, on Irish Cap. He beat fellow American Michael Plumb on Good Mixture and Britain's Hugh Thomas, who rode Playamar. The Americans also took the team title. It would have been a different

---

*Four of the best, the Americans Michael Plumb (Good Mixture), Denny Emerson (Victor Dakin), Don Sachey (Plain Sailing) and Bruce Davidson (Irish Cap), after winning the World Team Championship at Burghley in 1974*

Above: *The style of a dual world champion – American Bruce Davidson and Might Tango in Lexington 1978. Four years earlier he had won Burghley and his first world title on Irish Cap*

Right: *A Dane at Burghley – Nils Haagensen with Monaco*

story, though, had the Queen's horse Columbus not become lame at a crucial point in the trials. The big grey gelding held a commanding lead after the cross-country, but, just when the Queen and her son-in-law must have thought that Columbus was on his way to a World victory, Phillips had to withdraw him, and the title went to Davidson.

Four years after that, Bruce Davidson rode Might Tango to retain his World title in the heat of Lexington, beating John Watson of Ireland on Cambridge Blue, and West Germany's Helmut Rethemeier on Ladalco.

Although that 1974 Burghley will probably never be forgotten by the Queen and Captain Mark Phillips, Princess Anne has every reason to have fond memories of Burghley because, in 1971, she won the European Championship there on Doublet. It was one of the best things that could have happened to eventing, suddenly giving the sport the prominence it deserved. No other country in the world could boast a Princess who could take on and beat some of the best riders in the world at the toughest of equestrian sports.

Lucinda Green, too, has happy memories of Burghley, winning the second of her European titles there on George in 1977, beating Karl Schultz of West Germany on Madrigal.

There is no doubt that Burghley has seen some great sporting occasions, and some brilliant performances by horses and riders. It has even played its part in helping to create the greats. That is why the future of Burghley is assured, thanks to the hard work, and the vision, of those who make the trials possible year after year.

It is fitting that a man like Charles Stratton should be running them; he wants to make Burghley the best ever and, God willing, he will do just that because he believes so passionately in his work. He deserves success perhaps more than most, having had the courage to fight his way back from ill-health. A man such as Stratton does not give up easily – like his beloved Burghley Horse Trials, he is a winner.

Left: *Lucinda Green won her second European title at Burghley in 1977 on George*

Opposite above: *A moment of history and a family reunion – Princess Anne presented with her trophy by the Queen and Prince Philip after winning the European Championship at Burghley in 1971*

Above top: *Early morning blues and mist at Burghley*

Above: *Happiness at Burghley, 1983 – John Burbidge and wife Janet after an entertaining day*

# 7
# One Day at a Time

One-day horse trials are such a well-supported and growing part of the British scene that it is difficult to remember that they have, in this country, a history of only just over thirty years, shorter even than that of three-day events. Is it not ironic that while Britain has been overtaken in many of the sports it invented, soccer and cricket for example, it has proved pre-eminent in one which was imported?

Although the origins of three-day events were fairly widespread, Switzerland can fairly claim to have created one-day horse trials, in Thun, in 1922, and staged them regularly thereafter. And the Swiss had had two-day trials even before that. Switzerland was perhaps the most active country of all in pre-war days, at one-, two- and three-day-event level, including internationals.

In Britain the one-day did not start until after the Second World War, and then in a fragmented sort of way so that there is inevitably some disagreement as to what exactly was the first event to be held in this country. Some credit in this direction must certainly go to Lieutenant Colonel Bob Brackenbury, of Wellesbourne, Warwickshire, a site which has popped up intermittently over the years and has recently been revived again. Colonel Brackenbury ran a competition in 1946 which followed, at least in outline, the familiar formula: it consisted of a dressage test, which he created himself, a three-quarter-mile cross-country and then show jumping.

Because it was only part of a horse show some purists dismiss it, though until very recently Badminton also included show-jumping competitions, and Burghley

still does, and no one would question the credentials of such events as these. The winner of that competition at Wellesbourne was Mrs Lorna Johnstone who, twenty-six years later, rode for Britain in the dressage at the Munich Olympics when she was the oldest competitor in any sport, celebrating her seventieth birthday during the Games.

Colonel Brackenbury's event was intended as a sort of training run for the 1948 Olympics, held in Britain, but produced little response. After the Games, however, and especially once Badminton was firmly established, the one-day sport began to take off: indeed Colonel Brackenbury had offered to run one before the first Badminton, in 1949, but the British Horse Society did not want to get involved in anything that would take attention away from the three-day event.

Another early one-day trial was run by Henry Wynmalen, whose books of instruction rank as the most significant of any written by a British horseman, at Ewelme, Oxfordshire. It was run over the hunter trial course of the Woodland Hunt, of which Wynmalen was the Master, on 29 March 1950, but did not have any show jumping: there was a dressage phase, roads and tracks and then cross-country. As a trial for Badminton it was ideal – the dressage test was the same one – and of the twenty-two entries twenty were Badminton-bound. The winner was John Shedden on Golden Willow, who had won Badminton's first running in 1949. This was very much an official British Horse Society affair, with the Society providing the prize-money – £20 to the winner – and despite the lack of show jumping (or possibly because of it?) generally accounted a great success.

Tony Collings, whose Porlock training establishment was to become the headquarters of British eventing until his tragic death in 1954 in a Comet air crash, combined with Neil Gardiner to produce a set of rules under which one-day trials should be run, and presented them to the BHS late in 1949. Mr Gardiner offered to run a trial under these rules at his home at Great Auclum, near Reading, Berkshire, if the Society would underwrite them, but that the Society refused to do.

Mr Gardiner became one of the most influential men involved in horse trials in their formative years, and when the BHS – which remained equestrian sport's governing body, affiliated to the FEI (International

*Lorna Johnstone who helped to put British dressage on the map*

Equestrian Federation), until the formation of the British Equestrian Federation – decided to establish a Combined Training Committee in 1952, he was its first chairman.

This committee was appointed to 'direct all forms of Combined Training and to make rules and regulations'. Initially it was founded with a capital of £500 from the BHS, £500 from the Olympic Games and International Equestrian Fund, with a further £500 as a reserve against a possible loss by either Badminton or Harewood three-day events but, if not required, then for the use of the Combined Training Committee. In 1983 the sport was budgeting for well over a quarter of a million pounds, while in 1982, the last year of the Midland Bank's 'umbrella' sponsorship, their involvement was in excess of £300,000.

Colonel Brackenbury, ever persistent, ran his first 'proper' one-day event in the autumn of 1950 at Wellesbourne and continued to do so for the next decade. But what has become a familiar tale befell them the next year: it was due to be held in the spring, but had to be abandoned because of the bad weather. However, he staged one in the autumn, designed as a trial for the 1952 Olympic Games and incorporating a team competition, The Possibles v The Impossibles. The Possibles were chosen by Tony Collings, trainer and manager of the Olympic squad 'from those in training and others qualified for Helsinki'.

Mr Gardiner also, at last, was able to run his first horse trials at Great Auclum in the spring of 1951, organised by the Army Saddle Club, including Colonel Bill Lithgow. During the latter's many successful years as manager of the British team, they won the gold medals in Mexico and Munich. Gardiner and Tony Collings designed the cross-country course – which was built by the Army – and it was a great deal more demanding than those that had gone before, most of which were hunter trials courses or adaptations thereof. Collings had more experience than most of international and continental competitions, and knew that British riders would never learn the lessons needed to cope with courses they would meet abroad, especially in the Olympics, unless they had plenty of experience of them at home.

Not surprisingly, there were cries of alarm in abundance when the competitors walked the course, but Gardiner blunted all their arguments by riding it himself.

One-day events had established themselves quite firmly in the early 1950s, but even so only the very far-sighted could see how they would progress. At a meeting of the Combined Training Committee in 1953, it is reported in the minutes that 'the question of whether the British Horse Society should buy stop-watches was deferred'. What, I wonder, would they have said to today's electronic timing?

In 1953 eleven one- and two-day trials were scheduled, but it was not all roses: Stowell Park – another that has recently been revived – Gisburn, in Lancashire, and Wenlock all made a financial loss. Although most of the organisation was, as it still is, amateur, the need for a more professional 'headquarters staff' was understood, and Bill Thomson was employed as a 'show organiser', on a temporary basis in January 1953 and permanently just over a year later. Until his retirement just over a year ago Bill Thomson made an incalculable contribution, as course designer and builder, adviser and commentator at trials all over the country, including for many years at Burghley.

By October of 1953 the Combined Training Committee were agreed that there was sufficient support around the country to stage two events in one day, as long as they were geographically well spaced out, and it was also decided to split competitions into two classes, novice and open.

In 1954 the Calcutta Light Horse Trophy was initiated for the horse gaining most points during the season, and could not have had a more appropriate winner than Frank Weldon's Kilbarry, the first British event horse to reach the 'super-star' category. Kilbarry, who led the team that took the gold at the Stockholm Olympics, won the Trophy again in 1955, during which year he went through the entire season unbeaten; he won the European Championship at Windsor and also the three-day event at Harewood, hunter trials, show jumping and officer's charger classes as well as all the one-day trials he went in for.

Derek Allhusen, team gold and individual silver medalist in Mexico, has been especially successful in the Trophy, winning it in 1958 and 1959 with Laurien – dam of Laurieston who, owned by Major Allhusen and ridden by Richard Meade, won team and individual gold in Munich – and three times, in 1965, 1967 and 1968, with Lochinvar, his Mexico partner.

Although the one-day horse trial was originally intended as a training ground for the three-day event, and is of course still used as such by many, it has developed into a perfectly viable sport in its own right and it is an important element of the sporting spirit of horse trials that so many competitors have no ambition for major international honours. They like to get young horses, train them and then have them prove the efficacy of that training at novice or intermediate level, maybe not aspiring even to open classes. This was reflected when the Midland Bank came into the sport, bringing benefits

*Major Derek Allhusen teaming up with Lochinvar before the Mexico Olympics in 1968*

to a greater extent than perhaps any other sponsor has brought to any sport.

In 1968, the year before the Midland Bank, together with their Scottish counterpart, the Clydesdale, took over the financial support of almost all the one-day trials throughout the country there were twenty-nine one-day events. By 1982, the last year of their overall sponsorship, the number on the fixture list had grown to 114. In their first year, their involvement was around £30,000 – by the end it had grown to £350,000. And it was not just a financial involvement; their publicity department, by circulating all the national and local newspapers with information about each of the trials in turn, helped to create a public awareness of, and support for, one-day trials that has left them in their present healthy state despite the economic problems.

The Midland Bank's first championship – won by

Sarah Roger-Smith on Gambit – reflected the widespread interest in novice classes, and the novice championships, which fortunately are continuing, have since included such talented horses as Rachel Bayliss' Mystic Minstrel (1977), winner of the European Championship in 1983, and Michael Tucker's General Bugle (1981). Rachel's Gurgle the Greek looked for most of his career to be the archetypal 'one-day trials horse'. He was almost unbeatable, and notched up a tremendous amount of wins, including the points championship in 1975 and 1978, and yet seemed to find three-day events beyond him: he was even responsible for the creation of a new rule when, at Badminton, he went under a hanging log instead of over it!

Rachel and Gurgle the Greek won Chatsworth, which for many years rang down the curtain on the one-day season, no fewer than five times, but in 1978 Gurgle suddenly found his second wind: after finishing third at Burghley – and he would have won it but for a stop across country – he and Rachel triumphed at Boekelo, Holland, a month later. And in 1979 they took the silver medal in the European Championships. They are also on the role of honour, for 1976, of the Midland Bank Open Championship, among an auspicious cast that started in 1970 with The Poacher, originally ridden by his owner Martin Whiteley who, when back trouble forced him to give up, donated the horse to the Combined Training Committee. Richard Meade was his rider in 1970.

Other notable holders of the title have been Lucinda Prior-Palmer's Be Fair, Mark Phillips' Persian Holiday and dual winners John o' Gaunt, ridden by Richard Walker, in 1979 and 1980 – Walker also won in 1978 on Special Constable – and Virginia Holgate on Priceless in 1981 and 1982.

One of the greatest charms of one-day trials is the marvellous variety of different courses, often in the most beautiful of settings, from Penzance to Royal Deeside, from Chilham Castle in Kent to Tenby in West Wales. Some last only a few years, others, like Sherborne Castle, Dorset – built by Sir Walter Raleigh in 1594 – which began in 1952 and is the oldest to have run continuously since then, have a long and honourable history. It is an essentially individual sport, and so it was perhaps inevitable that sooner or later the Midland Bank's monopoly, beneficial though it had undoubtedly been, would come to an end.

The Bank is still involved, but at a much-reduced level, and trials around the country, aided by British Equestrian Promotions, the official body through whom most equestrian sponsorship is funnelled, had to find alternative sources of support from 1983 onwards. Despite the hard economic times the country is going through they have succeeded, and every month, sometimes every week, through the season announcements were made of new sponsors: some individual, some in 'packages' of several trials, but adding up to a healthy base from which the one-day sport can grow even more.

*Rachel Bayliss on Gurgle the Greek during the steeplechase phase at Badminton in 1978. For a long time they were almost unbeatable at one-day trials and won Chatsworth five times*

# 8
# The Windsor Trials

Hundreds of thousands of people visit Windsor each 'year to see the castle and if they are fortunate, to catch a glimpse of a member of the Royal Family. While the majority perhaps never achieve the latter, they are assured of a good time because Windsor is one of those delightful places with plenty of historic sights and many good restaurants. And, of course, it is also famous now for its show jumping and the three-day event which takes place in the Great Park.

The trials are run by Mrs Peggy Maxwell, a top businesswoman in London, who is also a very good dressage judge. How did she become interested in the rough and tumble world of eventing?

'I suppose when I ran the Pony Club as a district commissioner,' she says 'and my children were members. I began to run small Pony Club events, and then I moved on to staging a Pony Club area competition. After that my younger daughter qualified for Badminton. It was then I came to the conclusion that so many people who qualified for Badminton had never done any roads and tracks, never done steeple-chasing, and so James Grose, Bill Thomson and I got together and started the first two-day event at Crookham in the early sixties.'

That all worked well and then, eventually, Mrs Maxwell took over the Windsor trials and began building them up through much hard work and dedication. As with the major three-day events, as soon as one Windsor trial finishes, work begins in earnest on the next: it is a continuous process.

'I have a committee of twelve,' she says, and have two committee meetings a year – one in November and one in April – because I like everyone to know everyone else and get a team spirit going. The rest of the time I do everything with the managers of my different disciplines. I see them at various times and discuss any projects or problems that may have arisen.'

One of Windsor's plus factors over other events is having Princess Anne as president – and she is not merely a name on the event's list of officials.

'She is certainly not just a figurehead,' says Mrs Maxwell. 'She works extremely hard and has never missed a committee meeting yet. No matter how busy she is, she always manages to fit it in. For instance, when we cancelled in 1983 we had a meeting to discuss ploughing back the insurance proceeds into the course, so that we could drain the ground and make the fences more accessible. We spent two or three hours discussing that problem. She has never not come to a meeting when I have asked her to and she is consulted on everything we do. Princess Anne is extremely valuable to us because she knows eventing from the rider's point of view and, now, the organisers' side.'

Work, it seems, never stops and Mrs Maxwell can be proud that so much has been done at Windsor in such a short time. The land used for lorry parks has been drained and down towards the trade stands area a strip has been laid, called, aptly, 'Maxwell's Motorway'. The hard-core base is a great help to all concerned since any vehicle can be driven down it.

Good drainage is, of course, vital to any trials venue; if water cannot run off, the whole place obviously becomes like a quagmire which leads to events having to be abandoned.

At the time of writing the idea at Windsor is to have a blitz on the course, so that the weather cannot keep destroying everyone's hopes and plans. There is nothing worse for an organiser and committee to have worked hard all year and then be foiled by continuous rain, as happened in 1983.

Talking about her plans to beat the bad weather, Mrs Maxwell is highly enthusiastic, as she is in everything she does:

'With the fences that seem to be a bit boggy,' she says, 'we intend to put felting down, with scalpings on top of that and then turf on top of that – at take-off and landings – so that come what may we can still carry on. At one stage we had half done that, but there was so much rain we could not carry on with it.'

Once a trial has beaten the weather it must also attract trade stands and other business, so that it becomes a viable proposition and provides a service which the public wants. While some members of a family may be enthusiastic supporters of eventing, others only go along to keep them company, and trade stands and stalls are one way of keeping them happy. It is also a sure way for the show to bring in more much-needed money. After all, there is no point at all in keeping on with an event if, after the initial years, it makes no profit, or does not break even. If it is a failure, then everyone loses, including the riders and owners.

Mrs Maxwell, being a highly astute businesswoman, knows the value of trade stands. 'There is almost a waiting list and when I go to Burghley I walk around

*Windsor Castle provides a beautiful setting for the riders across country. Liz Braeck on Clowne*

them all and ask them if they are coming to Windsor. It is so important; I have someone solely in charge of trade stands and at first we did not charge them very much in order to get them in, and it has taken us five years to get things the way we want them. The fact that the event is held in Windsor Great Park certainly helped to influence things, there is no doubt about that.'

One reason why Windsor and many other events up and down the country are successful is because there is always an army of willing helpers ready to work and make sure that everything goes well.

'I had a list of fence judges from the days of Crookham,' Mrs Maxwell says, 'and because I judge a lot myself I see people who also offer their services. I have an annual list from which I work, but if anyone who works at the Windsor show is inefficient they do not last. I am very firm about that. Now we almost have a waiting list, because it is Windsor, of people who want to help. They do not even get expenses – just a bottle, or something – and we try and look after them the best we can while they are there. They are all volunteers and we just could not do without them. I suppose we have sixty-six fence judges, and about a dozen roads and tracks people.

'On cross-country day at Windsor we employ about 300 people, but not as many, of course, for the dressage and show-jumping days. They all have to be briefed and come along – doctors, vets and other experts – and the fences are explained to them, and they are told exactly what they have to do. That takes the whole of Friday afternoon and the following day they arrive at 8.00 a.m. I have only four paid staff, and the rest are purely voluntary.'

Mrs Maxwell, like everyone else connected with the trials, knows the strain of running an event, and the heartache that can sometimes go with it – right up until the final moments things over which the organiser simply has no control can still go wrong. It can be a nail-biting time and it pays to keep calm.

'Once the horse trials have started,' she says, 'everything is automatic, or should be, and that is not so bad as far as getting tired is concerned. It is the actual lead-up to the event months before that is the permanent worry, and you are always hoping that you will get the entries and everything will be all right. On the other hand, you can have far too many entries and then have to restrict some of them.'

For any show to be a success, the director and committee must make sure that the public is kept informed. To stage such an event and not do anything to attract the public would be foolish. That is why a great deal of

thought, and money, goes into advertising, so that come the day, people will turn up to watch the proceedings. The equestrian press as a whole does a fine job where this is concerned, many of them writing previews about a show, informing people who is going to be there, and what it will be like. That in itself is advertising, and it is a good thing, because it does, of course, promote the sport and public interest. After that it is self-generating.

'We advertise in *Horse and Hound*, the Burghley programme, and Frank Weldon is very kind and gives us advertising, of a quarter of a page, in the Badminton programme. We also have adverts in the local and national press, which is very expensive, and anywhere else we think might be beneficial.'

So far those have proved to be shrewd moves because the Windsor trials are very popular and interest in them is growing each year. For any sporting event to be a success, it must first attract the public and then give people good entertainment and value for money. Windsor's formula seems to fit the bill admirably.

But although things have gone very well for Mrs Maxwell, there must have been bad times, too. What has been her worst moment?

'There has been one such time,' she says, 'when we moved into the Great Park and everything was perfect until the day before the event. And then it absolutely poured down. At the time, I was sitting in the secretary's box and remember saying very firmly to myself, "We are not cancelling now, everything is ready and we are jolly well going on no matter what." That was a nasty moment.'

Her determination paid handsome dividends because the next three days were perfect, the show went on and everyone was happy with the result. But it could so easily have been called off had she given in to the rain.

'In 1980 it got very hard, and we had to rotovate; then, in 1981, everything was going well when there was a sudden downpour and we postponed the Windsor trials until after Bramham. Then, when that was on, I was on my own at Windsor because everyone had gone to Bramham and, when my own Range Rover got bogged, that was that – a washout.

'But it is not always like that; 1982 was a bumper year, no problems at all. It was a lovely few days and we had an increased number of spectators and everyone was happy with the new arena. Then, in 1983, we suffered like most other people after we had thirty-eight days of continuous rain.

'That was when even the grouter got stuck between two fences and I had to go and ring Princess Anne and tell her that the ground had got so bad I could not even get the tents up. As I have already said I never cancel anything until I have discussed it all with her, and told her what I am thinking of doing.

'Well, she had been there on the Thursday and so had a fair idea of what it was like and when I said, "Ma'am, it's now got far worse," she agreed that the show could not go on.'

Having fought the weather for several years and experienced the good and the not-so-good moments in three-day eventing, what is the major plan for Windsor?

'I hope that one day we might have a CCI there, but at the moment I believe Princess Anne feels that a standard event is very much needed at that particular time of the year – the end of May. So many people just getting over Burghley, come out of ordinary open events, to a slightly more difficult course, and so we think that they appreciate a standard event, which Windsor provides. But it would be great to have a CCI one day.'

*Princess Anne – enjoying herself at the Windsor Horse Trials of which she is President*

To stage any sporting show, however, costs a great deal of money and Windsor is no different from any other venue when it comes down to hard cash. It has to be found, because without the funds it would just not be possible to run an event. 'The first year you cannot count for us,' says Mrs Maxwell, 'because we started from scratch. But I would say that running the Windsor

Trials costs anything from £25,000 to £30,000. It is a lot of money, but that does include everything.'

It is a great responsibility but one which Mrs Maxwell and her team seem to cope with without any undue pressure. Indeed, they seem to take everything in their stride and carry on with undiminishing enthusiasm no matter what.

'I think the best time for us was in 1982,' she recalls, 'because there were no problems and everything was straightforward, including the weather. There was a happy atmosphere and that is what I like, and everyone enjoyed themselves. That is very important. Yes, that year stands out for me.'

But why does a lady like Mrs Maxwell want to run an event, even Windsor, when so much can go wrong, and the weather, over which there is no control, can destroy well-laid plans in just a few days?

'I rather like organising things and find it all a challenge. I think I inherited that from my father. And, although I am a businesswoman, I do love horse trials. I also judge a lot of dressage, both here and abroad – in Australia and New Zealand – and always do the three-day event in Sydney.'

Mrs Maxwell is a lady who never gives up. Even the foul weather which ruined many a sporting activity in 1983 never really got her down because, wisely, she had the show insured.

'Insurance is essential and even though we have only used it twice in seven years, it is a must. We even try and give the British Horse Society some money, apart from the £100 registration fee, and in 1981 they benefited because we gave them a certain amount from the insurance money.'

It would not, of course, have been the same large amount which Badminton and Burghley contribute, but every bit helps and it all adds up. That is just one of the reasons the British Horse Society is able to function properly – without financial help of this kind, large or small, it could not continue with its valuable work.

Eventing, and particularly the trials which take place at Windsor, is very lucky in that it has the backing of the Royal family, which generates public interest. Even if people do not know too much about the sport, they will still turn up to catch a glimpse of the Queen.

'There is no doubt about it,' says Mrs Maxwell, 'the Royal family, and in particular Princess Anne, has heightened the interest in eventing. It really is the same as what Prince Philip did for driving. People like to see the Royal family, and one of the main reasons they will make the trip to Windsor is because everything is informal, and the only way they notice the Queen is there is because there is usually a bevy of corgis somewhere nearby.'

Although Mrs Maxwell thinks a lot of the press, there are one or two people she does not care for too much, because they are not there primarily to cover the event but just to take as many pictures as possible of the Queen and her family.

She realises, however, that they are only doing their jobs and relates one story about several photographers who happened to be in her Mini-Moke one day when she was driving over the cross-country course.

'I was doing about thirty miles an hour,' she says, 'when suddenly one of them spotted Princess Anne. "Stop, stop," he yelled at the top of his voice and, knowing what they wanted, I put my foot down and carried on, thinking that would stop them. But they were not having any of that and, one by one, they bailed out over the side with their cameras. I was not worried about them at all because I had told them I did not want them chasing Princess Anne all over the place and as they decided to depart, in such an unorthodox manner, that was their problem.'

One person she is very grateful to in the media world is British Horse Society press officer Devina Cannon who, like Mrs Maxwell herself, loves eventing and the people in it. She has worked many long hours at shows and very much likes the Windsor trials, where she and her colleagues run the press tent. Results are always put up in near-record time and, if anyone wants to interview a rider, she produces them like magic. Devina believes passionately in what she is doing and is a great asset to any horse trials. She travels extensively from one end of the country to the other, even booking hotels for roving reporters on the way.

'We could not do without her,' says Mrs Maxwell. 'She always does a great job, and knows every member of the press. She, like me, knows that they are very much needed at events because we could not run horse trials without them. If sponsors did not continue to get publicity, they simply would not put money in to the events. It would all just stop. When we first started we had the Midland Bank and they were tremendous.

Now we have the TI Group and we had to get permission from the Queen to call them the TI Group Windsor Horse Trials. But that was perfectly all right and everyone is happy.'

To ensure that everything works smoothly, and to solve any problems that may surface during the trials, Mrs Maxwell starts at seven in the morning and is on hand until about seven-thirty in the evening. It can be a long, hard day.

Having been involved in the sport for many years, Mrs Maxwell thinks that eventing is going in the right direction and that there is no need for a drastic change.

'I think on balance the Horse Trials Committee run it all very well, and are doing a fine job, and I have great admiration for Martin Whiteley. He is always get-attable, and ready to listen to anything you have to say. When we were thinking of abandoning the Windsor Trials in 1983 I asked him to come over and have a look at the course and, although he had also to go to Chepstow, he was quite prepared to make both journeys. Nothing is ever too much trouble for him and that is why people like him so much.'

Among Britain's many event riders there are two whom Mrs Maxwell admires, not only because they

*Devina Cannon, press officer and great supporter of the Windsor Horse Trials*

are brilliant at what they do, but because they are never too busy to consider other people, no matter how much pressure they are under. They think it is important that others be considered apart from themselves and that is the mark of true champions. They are Richard Meade and Lucinda Green.

'I think one must admire Richard and Lucinda not only because both are very good competitors, but because they are also very reasonable, never complain and are capable of riding any horse well. Princess Anne is like that, too. You know, if you asked them to do their dressage test a little early, they would, and on occasions that can help you out.'

There are always many things to consider when running any sporting event and as far as horse trials are concerned the major point to remember is not to have the cross-country course built too big. Mrs Maxwell has no problems on that score because she enlisted the help of Bill Thomson.

'I have known Bill for many years,' she says. 'He was my course builder at Crookham and, in my opinion, is the best in the world. He has always been at my back, even when Hugh Thomas built the course, and he never ever overfaces a horse. I know Princess Anne was delighted when I asked him to build the course at Windsor, because she has a lot of time for him.'

Mrs Maxwell says that it costs between £300 and £400 to build each fence on the cross-country course,

and that there are always between twenty-eight and thirty fences to be built. They try to alter at least six obstacles every year and, in 1983, had changed a total of eight before the meeting was abandoned. In contrast to the cross-country fences, the steeplechase fences are mobile and the organiser can move them at will.

No matter how proud she is of the event Mrs Maxwell insists that it is the team around her who make it all work. She is quick to give credit where it is due, as in the case of deputy ranger Wiseman of Windsor Great Park:

'He is the most marvellous back-up,' she says 'and I just could not do without him. He is on the committee, runs the whole of that estate and nothing is ever too much trouble for him. There are, of course, many people to thank, including Brigadier and Mrs Eggar, who look after the dressage, and Phillip Wright, who is in charge of the show jumping.'

Everyone, in fact, plays a valuable part and, who knows, with a little luck and a lot of good weather, one day we might see the European Championships return to Windsor, where they were last held in 1955 and won by the then Major Frank Weldon, on Kilbarry.

They were not, of course, run at the present event; but, having been a guest at Mrs Maxwell's horse trials, I can see no earthly reason why they should not be: Windsor is run by a lady who is totally committed to what she is doing, and that is half the battle.

# 9
# The Pony Club ~Champions' Training Ground

For any nation to work its way to the top in eventing, and to make sure that it has the resources to stay there, requires long-term planning and a great deal of enthusiasm on the part of those running equestrian sport. If a country has one good rider with several good horses, it is possible for that country to win a championship, perhaps once, or even twice. But when those horses need rest, or time off to recover from injury, that country soon fades into obscurity: the only evidence that it was once a great eventing nation is an entry or two in the record books.

The answer, for any nation, lies with its young riders. If they are helped and trained at an early age, it will pay off in the long term. It is, however, all too easy to destroy their confidence or to fail to put a long-term plan into operation. Britain has the world beaten in this respect simply because the powers that be realised in good time that forward planning was essential and that looking after the young was vital to the future of equestrianism.

The officials certainly knew what they were doing and are to be congratulated for making it possible for Britain to lead the field in equestrian sport generally and eventing in particular. The key to success was the setting up of the British Horse Society Pony Club, whose executive officer, Lieutenant Colonel Bill Lithgow, is himself a former rider and *chef d'équipe* of British teams. He personifies all that is good about this organisation, which is perhaps the finest of its type anywhere in the world. At the helm you need men of experience and knowledge, like Major James Pinney, the Club's present chairman.

The main objectives of the Pony Club are to encourage young people to ride and learn to enjoy everything they do with horses. It teaches them how to behave

*Colonel Bill Lithgow – a moment for thought*

properly and to dress correctly for riding; and it aims to promote loyalty and good sportsmanship amongst its members. In fact, all things that are important in life. It is a measure of its success that lasting friendships have been formed at Pony Clubs all over the world.

Little did anyone realise that from the ranks of the Pony Club would spring so many top sportsmen and sportswomen, including World and Olympic champions. The secret lay in catching and encouraging their interest right from the start when Olympic medals and world fame were nothing more than dreams. But, for some, those dreams were to become reality and were to lead to a greatness that will never be forgotten by followers of sport.

It is interesting to note that the all-important workforce of the Pony Club very rarely shouts about the wonderful achievements of the youngsters in its care; those concerned just get on, quietly and efficiently, with the job in hand and when one lot of children eventually reaches adulthood, they take in and care for the next generation, ensuring the continuous process which helps keep Britain at the top of eventing. Those Pony Club organisers can feel justifiably proud of what they have done for sport and for the youth of this country.

Britain's Pony Club system is the envy of other nations, as Michael Bullen, himself a former Olympic rider, can testify: '"We wish we had the sort of organisation you have in the Pony Club," they say, because they know what it has done for our country.'

Among the famous names to have started in the Pony Club are Richard Meade, Bridget Parker, Mary Gordon-Watson and Captain Mark Phillips, all members of the British team which won the gold medals in the 1972 Munich Olympics.

*Captain Mark Phillips, Mary Gordon-Watson, Richard Meade and Bridget Parker celebrate with champagne after winning the team gold medal at the 1972 Munich Olympics. All were former members of the Pony Club*

*Michael Bullen on Sea Breeze, a former Olympic rider and a man who knows how important the Pony Club is to the young*

Apart from those gold medallists at Munich, Britain has a World Champion, Lucinda Green, who also started her remarkable career with horses in the Pony Club. Lucinda is a brilliant horsewoman and a great credit to the sport.

But why is the Pony Club so good at turning out champion after champion? What is the secret of its success? The plain truth is, organisation and unstinting willingness by those connected with the Club to help others, at whatever cost to themselves. The army of helpers outside headquarters, who run the local branches and regular shows, are tremendously generous; so too are the judges, course builders, car park attendants, tea makers and general runarounds who often give their services free, just to make sure the youngsters – some talented and others perhaps not so talented – have a fair deal and plenty of much-needed encouragement. Without their efforts the whole thing would not be possible.

One of the good points about the Pony Club – and there are many – is that it does not concentrate on one area of riding. Each year it stages championships for polo, dressage, show jumping and horse trials, plus both a boys' and girls' tetrathlon, and a mounted games championship. This means that every possible taste in equestrianism is catered for and there is no reason for any young person interested in riding to be left out.

Each Pony Club branch covers a specified area and each is looked after by a district commissioner, who in turn is helped by a local committee. To promote keenness amongst its membership, inter-branch competitions are encouraged which lead to a will to win, particularly in the Mounted Games Championship, which has a final at Wembley's Horse of the Year Show in October. This particular event, and the qualifiers leading up to the championship, are organised by the Pony Club and sponsored by the *Daily Mail* and Spillers.

No one who has seen the Prince Philip Cup final at Wembley could fail to be impressed by the whole incredibly exciting event – the teams of children dashing from one end of the arena to the other, seemingly totally out of control. Nothing, however, could be further from the truth: they train for months and, by the time they enter the arena, they know exactly what they, and their ponies, can do. There can, of course, be only one winner and for those who lose there are sometimes tears of frustration and excitement. But it is all good fun and, above all, character building.

Princess Anne was a member of the Garth Pony Club when she first started out, while Captain Mark Phillips belonged to the Beaufort. Little did they, or anyone else, know then that one day they would marry. It just proves that, more often than not, those who do fall in love have the same interests. In their case it was horses. During his time with the Pony Club, Captain Phillips rode for the Beaufort horse-trials team and so began an interest, and a devotion to the sport, that was to make him an Olympic team gold medallist and, eventually, the only man to win Badminton four times.

During those early times in their respective Pony Clubs, they both had falls from ponies and were beaten more often than they won – Princess Anne had one pony who would do everything once and that was all! They both knew what it felt like to be also-rans, and it did them no harm at all. It was during his trials days at Pony Club level that Phillips met two men who were to play a significant part in his success story. They were Colonel Frank Weldon and Alec Scott, both experts in their field. Weldon, the man who runs Badminton, won a team gold medal in the Stockholm Olympics in 1956, riding Kilbarry, so meeting him was the best thing that could have happened to an aspiring three-day-event rider. Before Weldon, Alec Scott had helped Phillips with his dressage and show jumping, and Molly Sivewright, one of Britain's top dressage trainers, also gave him tremendous help and encouragement.

All this serves to highlight the fact that having help in those formative years is of vital importance. Nobody can say that Captain Phillips would not have won all he has if he had not been helped as a youngster. But the plain fact is that assistance was available from some very experienced and talented people who cared about the young riders and were good enough to give of their time. There is nothing better than experienced tuition when you are trying to be good at what you do; the only way to learn is to listen and make a mental note of what is said. And what could be better for an event rider than to be listening to Colonel Frank Weldon? A highly talented rider, he has done more in the world of eventing than most people will ever aspire to, and he has a wealth of knowledge, both in and out of the saddle.

It is because of people like him that Britain has attained such heights in the sport and why we quite often beat the world. And if that statement seems nationalistic, it is – we happen to be proud of what our riders, and everyone connected with them, have achieved.

Another man who has had much to do with the British Horse Society Pony Club is Raymond Brooks-Ward, one of Britain's top television commentators, managing director of British Equestrian Promotions and the person in charge of the Pony Club teams which take part in the Prince Philip Cup for the Pony Club Mounted Games Championship at Wembley. The youngsters love him. He has this to say:

There is no doubt in my mind that the Pony Club provides a basis for sound riding techniques and teaches youngsters to love their ponies and look after them. The Pony Club treats that very seriously and is the grounding for many young people of comradeship and so much success. They are taught to compete, rather than set out to do others down, and that is very important for character building, not only for event riders but everyone. I first became involved with the Prince Philip Cup in 1960 and everyone who competes in that knows that it is team spirit that counts. You have only to see the kids at Wembley, living together, helping each other, even though they are riding against each other, to know what I mean. Again, the team spirit comes through, and always will do if youngsters are taught properly at an early age.

Early on, the Mounted Games were heavily criticised by some people, who thought the ponies were being pulled about too much during the competition. But no harm has ever come to them and Brooks-Ward is well aware of the situation. 'Some people did make contact with us over that,' he said, 'but the ponies are perfectly all right and when they are twisting and turning, they are teaching the children balance.'

A love of ponies and riding can be instilled in children at a very early age. Pony Club branches run camps during the summer holidays, members sometimes living under canvas. During the day those in charge organise activities such as rallies, gymkhanas and visits to hunting yards. This means that all the while the youngsters are at camp they are thinking about ponies or riding them, and learning to live and share with each other.

That is when children who have a genuine feel or talent for riding are able to develop it, because the general surroundings are right, they are happy and they are doing what they love most. They have the opportunity of finding out exactly what they want to do, and they are encouraged to do it. Just think what might have happened if people like Richard Meade and Captain Mark Phillips had spent most of their time playing rugby or football instead of going to rallies and gymkhanas. Eventing would have been the poorer for it. They played those sports, but horses, thank goodness, were their first love.

That is why the Pony Club plays such an important role, since it caters for practically all equestrian interests. Polo, for example, once considered to be a rich man's sport, is anything but nowadays. Any boy or girl with a pony can go on courses and eventually play the game within the actual Pony Club. The point is that interest in riding is maintained and the youngsters are not lost to equestrian sport through being diverted to other pastimes. There is an old saying that if you get them when they are young, you have them forever. That is certainly true with horse sports.

Ask any of the top riders today what they thought of their Pony Clubbing days and the answer in practically every case would be affectionate, because it was always great fun and in the quiet of the night, after a particularly good effort at the local show, one could go to bed dreaming that the winner's rosette nestling under the pillow might one day turn, like magic, into an Olympic gold medal! Dreams, yes, but for some those gold medals do become a reality, and with them come the pride and thanks of a nation.

The great plus factor, as far as the Pony Club is concerned, is that it makes available to youngsters who like horses the very things they want. That is why having branches all over the country is such a good idea. Even if, in a particularly built-up area, facilities such as woodland or fields are not easily obtainable for riding purposes, the Pony Club organisers will always find other ways of encouraging their members. Film shows and lectures are provided and well-known riders and equestrian personalities are always willing to give talks and encouragement to the young who, one day, may want to follow in their footsteps. Again, it is the all-important thread of continuity right down the line.

Many of the thousands of people who make all this possible, working countless hours for the good of the Club, never get the praise they deserve from the equestrian public at large. That does not seem to worry them unduly and they carry on with their good work regardless. But if they did not put in the time, and the effort, some of the small branches around the country could not operate to capacity. These people really are the unsung heroes on whom everyone relies so much.

One such lady is Mrs Clare Scowen, from Chislehurst, in Kent, who has been connected with the Pony Club as an unpaid helper and in many different capacities since 1947. She was an area organiser of the North West Kent branch for eleven years and treasurer for ten. She is much admired for all the hard work she has put in, and the help and encouragement she has given to the youngsters. Even now, in her early seventies, she is always available for help and advice and says, 'I always liked anything to do with horses, but when I finished as area organiser, I did not want to outstay my welcome.' In fact, that would never have been the case because everyone admired her for what she had done over the years.

'Apart from enjoying the whole thing,' she adds, 'it does one's ego good, and gives one a huge amount of satisfaction. And being with children always keeps one young. It is I who should thank the Pony Club.

'Perhaps the best thing about it all is when you have taught a youngster to ride and he, or she, then ends up representing Britain. That gives you a warm feeling. Another important aspect, and perhaps the one I like best of all, is that being involved with the Pony Club gave me the opportunity of helping the less fortunate children, the youngsters who did not have ponies.

'Riding and the Pony Club have been in my family for years, and for as long as I can remember we have had something to do with it. I suppose you can say I was bred to it, because my father and sisters all did their bit with the Pony Club and it just carried on to me.

'It does the children a lot of good to belong to it, and when the Pony Club held its jubilee, you should have seen the champions, from eventing, dressage and show jumping, who turned up there.

'But the thing I will never forget is when I had two very bad hips and was due to go into hospital for an operation. When I rode, I had to be assisted from the saddle and one day, when I returned to the stables, one of the children said, "I'll help Mrs Scowen off today." Those few words will stay with me for the rest of my life. Because the child who said it cared.'

Lieutenant Colonel Bill Lithgow is one of the men who has helped the Pony Club tremendously and, as executive officer, knows exactly what is needed to keep things running smoothly. After the Second World War he taught at Sandhurst, did a spell of soldiering in Egypt, was several years with the King's Troop and the 10th Hussars and finally went to Aden. It was in Aden that, while sitting in his office, he received a long, type-written envelope. 'I thought it was from my bank manager,' laughs Bill, and duly left it unopened for two weeks. But when I did finally get round to it, it was from "Babe" Moseley, asking if I would like to manage the British eventing team.'

*The late Lieutenant Colonel 'Babe' Moseley*

He finally accepted the offer and just a year later was taking a squad to ride in Russia. They had great success under his direction. Bill, in fact, himself rode eventing in the early fifties. 'It was nothing like it is now,' he adds, quickly. 'But I did compete at Badminton.'

On one of these occasions, when he was planning to set off the next day, his wife woke him up at 4.30 a.m. to tell him that their baby was due to arrive at any moment. 'So I whisked her into hospital, hitched up my trailer, went to Badminton and returned to inspect the baby.'

That was typical of the man: he never panics, always has everything under control, and is liked by all who come into contact with him. When he was managing the British team, he was never too busy to talk to the press, and had the enviable ability of making total strangers feel completely at ease in his company. There could not have been a better man to run the Pony Club, and he has no doubt that this organisation is one of the reasons Britain does stay at the top.

'I am certain of it,' he says, 'and I know that we play a significant part in the training and development of young riders. One of the reasons for this is that being a member of the Pony Club gives them the opportunity of getting instruction from people who know what they are doing. It is also, of course, tremendous fun, and the Pony Club branches hold competitions in which members can ride. Where would those children who are interested go if there was not a local branch of the Pony Club available to them?'

Listening to Bill Lithgow fills you with confidence for Britain's equestrian future, because he has no doubts whatsoever that everything, as far as our youngsters are concerned, is going to plan.

The Pony Club has been such a great success here that many other countries have set up branches and have affiliated themselves to the parent body in Britain. 'We have about 350 branches here,' Bill says, 'but not all of them run an event team. Many do, however. The Americans have a flourishing Pony Club now, and so do other countries, but they all stem from ours, particularly those in the Commonwealth countries.

'Perhaps the most encouraging signs are seen when one looks at the list of nations who have set up their own Pony Clubs and are following Britain's lead. They include Australia, Cyprus, Botswana, Ethiopia, Hong Kong, Japan, Barbados and many others. They incorporate the basic principles and adjust everything in order to suit local conditions. We have no control over them after that.'

But it is when Bill gets down to the objects of the Pony Club that you can understand why it means so much to him, and to all the others who have helped to make Britain great in the equestrian world.

The Pony Club sets out: 'To encourage young people to ride and learn to enjoy all kinds of sport connected with horses and riding; to provide instruction in riding and horsemanship; to instil in members the proper care of their animals and to promote the highest ideals of sportsmanship, citizenship and loyalty, thereby cultivating strength of character and self-discipline.'

When Bill has finished telling you about the objects of the Pony Club, you feel good, and you realise that, if everyone lived by such conduct, the world would be a much better place.

For children, of course, the training and the principles behind it are right. Once the youngsters have been taught, they become much better people and, most certainly, thinking and considerate riders. Anyone who has ever seen a British three-day-event team will know exactly what is meant by discipline: win or lose, their attitude towards their rivals and the sport remains the same. They treat both with respect, and that is exactly how it should be.

Lessons can easily be learned from places like Badminton, and Burghley, when the winners finally leave the arenas, sampling the sweet taste of success. The first to congratulate them are the losers, which says a lot for the sport, the people in it and everyone in the Pony Club branches all over Britain who played a part in teaching their members to be decent human beings. And, with a firm foundation like that, a nation must have every chance of proving its worth at all times.

# 10
# Lady in a Million

Lucinda Green, World Champion; the only rider ever to have won the European Championship more than once; or to have won Badminton five times, and each on a different horse. Thinking up new superlatives to describe her performances, and her personality, has stretched our vocabularies increasingly since, at the age of just nineteen, she and her beloved Be Fair triumphed at Badminton in 1973.

It has been the sort of story admired by our grandmothers: attractive, good-natured girl, youngest daughter of retired Major General Erroll Prior-Palmer and the Lady Doreen, buys a horse no one else wanted, and through sheer hard work and grit, urged on by her loving but realistic family, turns the rebellious chestnut into a champion. Fine, stop there. If it had been fiction, many readers would no doubt have said it was all just a little too good to be true. But that is just the first part of the story.

To go on and win Badminton four more times, and another European Championship – on a horse that had gained himself a well-earned reputation for tripping over fences. Marry a handsome Australian: win a World title with a horse which, the autumn before, nearly died of travel-sickness. Tragedy too, at the death of her father. Nearly have to quit because the financial strain of it all is just too much; find a sponsor, John Burbidge's SR Direct Mail, who makes it possible to continue, and immediately repay him by her record-breaking fifth Badminton success.

And John Burbidge's part in it sounds like a fairy story itself – son of a South London bricklayer, who at fourteen, worked as a newspaper packer and after doing the same job in the direct mail company, worked his way up to become its chairman! Receiving the coveted Whitbread Trophy from the Queen. Oh, really! No one is going to believe all that. But it's true. So where do fiction writers go from there?

In 1983 Princess Anne made a very important point when, talking about the lack of top-class young event riders, she said that the trouble with most of them was that they were over-indulged, had the choice of too many horses and so, when something went wrong with one of them, he or she would switch to another instead of concentrating on that one and trying to find out why it was misbehaving, and then effecting a cure. She pointed out that most of the top riders had reached the pinnacle with just one good horse, and only when the lessons were learned and the heights had been scaled, at least a good part of the way, did they spread their talents more widely. Lucinda was one of the riders she gave as an example, and how appropriate a choice she was.

Lucinda's parents bought Be Fair for her fifteenth birthday, 7 November 1968, for £525, and within a few weeks would have taken a hundred pounds loss if they had been able to find a buyer, so difficult a horse was he. But they persevered, and although Be Fair was never an easy horse he was undoubtedly a brilliant one, and his rider's determination took him to the top just as surely as he took her there.

Be Fair came into the Prior-Palmer household by way of an advertisement in *Horse and Hound*: he was the only son of Sheila Willcox's good event horse Fair and Square – who won Burghley the same year, 1968 – and who as a precocious two-year-old leaped into an adjoining field and had an unplanned assignation with the Thoroughbred mare Happy Reunion. Be Fair had already been rejected as 'too nappy' by one experienced trainer looking for an event horse, and had a badly scarred leg as the result of an encounter with wire, but when Lucinda first rode him she felt there was something special.

The Prior-Palmers have always been a close-knit family, all of them involved in the activities of each other – I shall never forget the army of tee-shirts with 'Be Fair' printed on them in Kiev when Lucinda made her first attempt at the European Championship – but luckily her father was away in Australia on business when she and her mother went to inspect Be Fair or he would probably never have been bought. Lady Doreen was swayed by her daughter's enthusiasm and the deal, with some misgivings, was done.

Lucinda was away at school when she received the birthday telegram that told her Be Fair was hers, and by the time she went home for the Christmas holidays letters had already warned her that her 'first real horse' was a problem.

She had been taught to ride since she was four at a nearby riding school run by Mrs Betty Skelton, going out with the local hunt, the RA (Salisbury Plain), on a leading rein and graduating through a series of bigger ponies until the arrival of Be Fair. He, too, was at livery with Mrs Skelton. When Lucinda took him out for the first time he 'spooked' at every sweetpaper, whipped round on the road and, after jumping a small cross-country practice fence twice, refused so adamantly to do so again that he reared and went over backwards.

Friends were brought in to help, and Be Fair was 'encouraged' to go forwards, rather than sideways, backwards or even skywards, by being closely pursued by a Land-Rover with a lungeing whip projected suggestively from a window. In his early days he would even lie down when bored with being lunged in circles. He was enough of a character to test anyone's patience and ingenuity, and in overcoming his quirks, or at least

*John Burbidge, Lucinda Green and husband David celebrating the world champion's birthday with greetings from sponsor SR Direct Mail*

reducing them to a manageable level, Lucinda learned lessons that were to prove invaluable with the many other horses she was to ride to success.

Concentrating on one horse may be the way to the top, but once a rider has reached the peak a constant supply of good horses will be needed to stay there. Many riders, perhaps the majority, have their greatest achievements on just one horse, and as he gets older, so their triumphs diminish: each of Lucinda's five Badminton successes have been on different horses, she has won the European Championship twice on different horses and the World title on a third. Greater versatility would be difficult to imagine.

But, in those early days with Be Fair, all that was still to come. Tom Payne gave the horse valuable schooling hunting with the Pytchley while Lucinda was still at school, but she was able to get weekends at home and rode him much more often. Then, as later, she went to the best teachers she could find, Dick Stillwell, Pat Burgess, David Hunt, and still, naturally, Betty Skelton: this has been her maxim throughout her career, never to think that she 'knew it all' but always to try and find the expert in whatever field was worrying her most. Stillwell, who has also trained riders such as Richard Meade and Mary Gordon-Watson, told Lucinda when he was training her in her pony days, 'Never stay in one place, Lucinda. Go and learn as much as you can from as many people as'll teach you.'

Lucinda's and Be Fair's first official British Horse Society horse trial, in the wake of various Pony Club outings, was at Rushall in the spring of 1970. After three such outings they came to the notice of the late Colonel 'Babe' Moseley, one of the great characters of British eventing, whose particular brief was chairman of the junior selectors. He wanted them in the trial, to be held in conjunction with Tidworth three-day event, for the British team for the European Junior Championships. Lucinda's first attempt at a three-day event, and her back-up team's approach to getting horse and rider fit enough, was a trial-and-error affair; but it worked, and despite an attack of German measles just before Tidworth she and Be Fair went well enough to please both her and her parents. They pleased Colonel Moseley, too, but not enough to get into the team. 'More experience needed' was the verdict and that was what Lucinda and the *équipe* Prior-Palmer set about acquiring.

It was not easy, not always pleasant – as when Be Fair fell and had to be pulled by his tail from under a fence – but gradual progress was made, especially with help from David Hunt in the ever-fraught territory of the dressage arena. And in 1971 came their first selection for a British team, and one moreover which brought the European Junior Championships to Britain for the first time. Although Lucinda and Be Fair were eleventh individually, this was the first time they had ever had a winner's rosette; what prescience the mayor of Wesel, the West German town where the Championships were held, must have had when he told a fractious Be Fair he would 'have to get used to it'. Next time out, at the Cullompton one-day trials, they scored their first individual success.

There are some horses, special horses, who simply cannot be bothered to concentrate or exert themselves over small fences and on minor occasions, but will perform wonders when the questions asked measure up to their capacity. Marion Coakes' Stroller was one: no more than moderate in junior pony classes, but capable of winning a World Championship and an Olympic silver medal. So Be Fair showed himself to be: he was in his element at Badminton, most dramatic of all the regular three-day events, with huge crowds thronging the lovely park: Lucinda, aged eighteen, and he had their first outing there in 1972, and despite a run-out at Tom Smith's Walls when the reins slipped through her hands, finished fifth – and were put on the short-list for the Munich Olympic Games.

The name Lucinda Prior-Palmer was becoming public property, newspaper and television cameras came to put the Hampshire girl on record. Looking back later Lucinda said that she found the experience with the television cameras hopelessly frightening; how much that has changed, for there is now no better spokeswoman, or man, than she for the sport which has done so much for her, and for those principles by which she and her parents have lived. When it was decided that, because of the Russian invasion of Afghanistan, no British equestrian team would go to Moscow – a decision with which most of the other Western nations concurred – Lucinda's outspoken support was immediate and forthright.

Most years the short-list for an Olympic Games or a championship diminishes through the season, as horses go lame or lose form, but in 1972 all ten stayed sound, and Lucinda was left out of the side that won both the team gold and, via Richard Meade and Laurieston, the individual gold as well. Four years later, in Montreal, they were included, in what was destined to be just about the unhappiest chapter of Lucinda's competitive life.

But there was glory to come first, starting in 1973

---

Opposite: *Left hand down and ever onward – Captain Mark Phillips on Lincoln at the Badminton Horse Trials*

Above: *Gold medals galore as the British team – Rachel Bayliss, Lucinda Green, Virginia Holgate and Richard Meade – complete a victory gallop after winning the World title at Luhmühlen in 1982*

Left: *Her Royal Highness Princess Anne has a lucky escape as Stevie B falls in the water at Badminton. The horse has since been sold*

Right: *Proud moment in the life of John Burbidge, Chairman of SR Direct Mail, as he collects the Whitbread Trophy from Her Majesty the Queen after Regal Realm had won Badminton in 1983*

Below: *Riding into history – Lucinda Green and Regal Realm after winning the World Championship in Luhmühlen, 1982*

Left: *One way to jump out of water – Clarissa Strachan and Merry Sovereign negotiate the boat at Badminton in 1980*

Above left: *The trials and tribulations of a three-day event rider are vividly portrayed by Joanna Winter on Stainless Steel as they take a horrifying fall at the log*

Above: *Riding through the reeds at Burghley, Jane Holderness-Roddam and Warrior show how it should be done*

Above right: *Kim Walnes and The Gray Goose having trouble at Badminton, 1983*

Right: *Up, up and away – Michael Tucker and General Bugle in action at Badminton in 1983. They eventually finished second to Lucinda Green and Regal Realm*

Left: *Fiona Moore and Squire's Holt, winners at Boekelo, Holland, in 1981. Their tenth place at Badminton, 1983, qualified them for the European Championships shortlist, but Fiona was injured in a fall the day after the shortlist was announced*

Above left: *Diana Clapham and Windjammer sail over a steeplechase fence during the European Championships at Frauenfeld, 1983*

Above: *Lizzie Purbrick and Felday Farmer jump boldly into the lake at Badminton*

Above right: *Richard Walker and Ryan's Cross, winners of Windsor and Burghley three-day events in 1982*

Right: *Determination etched on Lucinda Green's face as she takes Regal Realm clear in the show-jumping phase of the 1983 European Championships to clinch the silver medal*

Far right: *Princess Anne, first member of the British royal family to ride in an Olympic Games, and Goodwill during an eventful cross-country at Montreal. Despite a fall, they finished the course*

*A proud moment in history as the Queen presents the silver
bowl to Lucinda Green after she had won Badminton for a
record fifth time. The Duke of Beaufort (left), Prince Philip and
John Burbidge look on*

when Lucinda notched the first of her five Badminton
successes – perhaps one should say five, so far! It was a
tough cross-country course for a post-Olympic year,
with only thirty finishers from sixty-nine starters, but
Be Fair, equal fourth after the dressage, had the fastest
clear round across country and was clear show jumping,
too, to win by more than twenty penalty points from
Munich gold medalist Richard Meade on Barbara
Hammond's Eagle Rock.

As a result they were included in the British team for
the European Championships, to be held in Kiev, in the
Ukraine. By a strange quirk, it was not Lucinda's first

Opposite: *Rachel Bayliss and Mystic Minstrel, who finally got
their act together to win the European Championship at
Frauenfeld, Switzerland, in 1983*

visit to this historic Soviet city; she had been there on a
package holiday with a friend a couple of years earlier.
This was no happy return, marking as it did the end, at
least temporarily, of an amazing run of British success
that included the three previous European Championships, the World Championship in 1970 and the Olympic
golds in Mexico and Munich. With Princess Anne
going to defend the individual title she had won two
years earlier, the spotlights of publicity on the British
team were at their brightest.

The second fence at Kiev will go down in eventing
history as one of the sport's major disasters; walking the
course beforehand it was clear that it would be, but there
seemed no sensible, safe way to jump this huge parallel
over a ditch at the bottom of a steep mound. Janet
Hodgson had a horrific fall there with Larkspur, some-
how went on, fell again later and still finished the
course; Princess Anne fell, and limped away; Debbie
West and her little Baccarat were eliminated there. The
only recipe for jumping it was the one Mark Phillips
had given to Lucinda before her first Badminton, 'keep
kicking'. And in this case get the whip out as well.

Lucinda and Be Fair went last for the team, and had to finish if the team was not to be eliminated. With all the considerable impulsion at her command, over they went – only to fall at another, fairly innocuous fence in the woods; but, they finished, and the British team came in third, behind Germany and the USSR, with one of the Russian riders, Alexander Evdokimov, the individual champion.

In the spring of 1974 Lucinda broke an arm riding in a point-to-point, a pursuit which gave her little enjoyment and an abiding admiration for National Hunt jockeys, and she and Be Fair had a spectacular fall at Badminton's new S-fence. She pursued her quest for knowledge by going to Germany for a course of training with Hans Günter Winkler, whose five Olympic show-jumping medals – four team, one individual – are a record in any branch of equestrianism. In her marvellous biography of Be Fair, *Up, Up and Away*, Lucinda wrote: 'My principal aim is to learn, in the end, how to ride. It is a simple philosophy. If every horse that a person sits on performs beautifully for him then presumably he can consider himself an artist. Maybe then any success that he enjoys is not gained through that transient quality luck, but through the imperishable quality of skill.'

Lucinda, a natural cross-country rider but by no means a 'natural' at either show jumping or dressage, has, by her absolute dedication and hard work, turned deficits to her advantage. Others with more inborn talent in these facets of equestrianism have, in the end, been overtaken.

The World Championships were held at Burghley that autumn, and Be Fair was a doubtful starter after being held up with leg trouble; in the end he went, as an individual, but Lucinda lost her way, and time, on the steeplechase and they finished only tenth.

By now Lucinda was riding other horses as well as Be Fair, including the ill-fated Wide Awake and the mare Ellie May, owned by Michael Naylor-Leyland, and she took all three to Badminton in 1975. It used to be possible to ride three horses round Badminton: now riders are limited to two, but neither Lucinda nor most other people were aware of the change. That year, at the end of the dressage, with Be Fair in the lead, Badminton was abandoned under a deluge of rain, and a potentially tricky situation was avoided.

It also left the selectors with a problem for the European Championships, but Be Fair won the final trial and was included. The interval training method of getting horses fit that Lucinda had adopted from the Americans, and Bruce Davidson in particular, was regarded as something cranky by most of the British camp, but it certainly worked for him. Third after the dressage, Lucinda and Be Fair ate up the beautifully

*The way to victory for Britain – Lucinda and Regal Realm at Luhmühlen, 1982*

*Winning team – David Green, groom Joanna Capjon and Lucinda with Regal Realm, at home in Appleshaw*

*Sitting well back but safe, Lucinda on Village Gossip at Fontainebleau in 1980*

built cross-country course at Luhmühlen in Germany; at that stage the British team led as well, but Sue Hatherly and Harley had a fall in the show jumping, putting the team back behind the USSR. Be Fair made no mistakes, and neither did Princess Anne, who took the silver on Goodwill.

The first of the peaks had been conquered, and the still unfinished tale ranges with Alpine-like splendour across the eventing scene, but with shadowy depths as well; such as when Lucinda's second Badminton success, on Wide Awake in 1976, turned sour as the horse collapsed and died in the arena after his first lap of honour. And later the same year at Montreal, when Be Fair ran in his last three-day event and broke down so badly it was even thought he might have to be put down. After a superb dressage he went round the Olympic cross-country course tremendously well, and then, just as Columbus had done when he and Mark Phillips had had the 1974 World Championship in their grasp, slipped a tendon off his hock and was crippled. Happily, his story did not end there, but back in his Hampshire home where he recovered sufficiently to be ridden and enjoy his declining days.

With Wide Awake Lucinda had already shown her ability to win with other horses, and in 1977 she had two totally different animals to ride, Charles Cyzer's Killaire, whose lack of natural athleticism made what he was to achieve, including a Badminton win in 1979, all the more remarkable, and Elaine Straker's George, a splendid-looking animal but with a proven tendency to fall. It was the first time she had ever ridden two horses round Badminton, and George, immaculately clear throughout, gave her her third Whitbread Trophy, with Killaire, who belied his looks across country but hit one show-jumping fence, third.

That summer Lucinda's father died of cancer. He was a man of outstanding qualities, with the ability to command that had made him a Major General in the 9th Lancers, combined with a down-to-earthness, and complete involvement in his youngest daughter's sporting career. Right up to the end he looked forward to her future, and, despite the loss she inevitably felt, Lucinda carried on, and rode George in the final trial for the European Championships, the Midland Bank Championships at Locko Park, just two days after his death. It nearly ended in disaster as an exhausted Lucinda was run away with: I shall never forget the sight of her galloping headlong down a long hill towards a water jump, clearly unable to steady George.

But they survived, and went on to win the European Championship at Burghley, which made Lucinda the first person ever to win two such titles, and the first to win Badminton and Burghley in the same year. And they did it even though Lucinda fell off in the steeple-chase, not at a fence, which would have in-1611curred penalties, but after George became entangled with one of the marker ropes. He dragged her along, at last stopped to let her remount, and still finished inside the time limit.

Conditions were changing in the eventing world, and while it remained still essentially amateur, the costs of keeping the number of horses that any rider must have were mounting inexorably, making it almost impossible to continue without a sponsor. That situation is accepted now; it was still something of a rarity in 1978, but Brian Giles wrote in the *Daily Mail* that Britain's double European Champion would probably have to quit, if she did not find a sponsor. Out of the subsequent publicity came an offer from Overseas Containers, a firm for which her father had once worked, and since then many other top riders have found similar supporters. The OCL sponsorship lasted for five years, but in the winter of 1982 Lucinda, with her husband David, found themselves again without backing, until John Burbidge's SR Direct Mail company came to the rescue.

Lucinda's first venture for OCL so nearly triumphed, when Village Gossip was second at Badminton, but their trip to Lexington, Kentucky, for the World Championships was as much a disaster for Lucinda as it was for most of the others. In the hot, humid atmosphere the course was too much, in particular the Serpentine fence where Gossip, and many others, fell.

The occasion exhausted Village Gossip as much as it did many of the horses that competed there, and 1979 was Killaire's year; but his Badminton success was followed by a disappointment at

*Yes, it has been a tiring day – Lucinda at Burghley after the cross-country*

*The style of a champion – Lucinda sits firm as Beagle Bay sprawls, Badminton, 1983*

the European Championships in Luhmühlen. At the end of the speed and endurance phase Lucinda and Killaire were lying third to the eventual winners, Nils Haagensen on Monaco, and the British team was leading. But Killaire was lame afterwards, and could not jump in the final phase, leaving Ireland to overtake Britain for the team title.

Killaire would have won Badminton a second time in 1980, but for a foot in the show-jumping water; and Village Gossip staged an amazing recovery at the Fontainebleau Festival that, for most of the Western world, replaced the ostracised Moscow Olympics. He was only sixty-fifth of sixty-nine starters, after the dressage, but still finished seventh. It was there, too, that Lucinda saw, and bought, Regal Realm from Australian Mervyn Bennett.

Her chance of a crack at the 1981 European title was frustrated when both her short-listed horses, Village Gossip and the ex-New Zealander Mairangi Bay, were injured at the final trial. And in the autumn Regal Realm was taken desperately ill on the journey back from Boekelo, Holland.

That December Lucinda married David Green, whom she had first met on one of her regular trips to Australia a few years earlier. Their base remained at Appleshaw House, with the horses still stabled there, although they moved into a small cottage in the village.

Regal Realm showed his resilience in the spring of 1982, winning a preliminary and then going round Badminton faster than any other horse has ever done to finish seventh, one place lower than husband David on Mairangi Bay, who has now become his regular ride.

Second place on Regal Realm in the final trial, the Midland Bank Championships at Locko Park, this time fortunately without the mishaps of 1981, confirmed their place in the World Championships team for Luhmühlen, and what happened there was the highest peak yet of Lucinda's career. Regal Realm was sixteenth after the dressage – with David, riding for Australia on Mairangi Bay, sixth after a superb test – then Lucinda, with the horse she now rates as better across country even than Village Gossip, had one of only four completely clear rounds in the speed and endurance to pull up to equal second. Germany's Helmut Rethemeier was in the lead, with Santiago, and the American Kim Walnes, riding in her first championship, was level with Lucinda on The Gray Goose.

So it all depended on the show jumping: The Gray Goose had one fence down, and dropped behind Regal Realm, who was clear again. Rethemeier and Santiago could afford to have one down and still win; right from the beginning they looked decidedly fallible; luck seemed at first to be with them, but then two fences fell and Lucinda Green was the new World Champion. Britain had regained the team title, as well, and the champagne flowed in abundance.

But when the fizzing stopped, Lucinda and David realised that all the glory in the world would not pay the feed bills. Overseas Containers, after a five-year period, had come to the end of their sponsorship, and, incredibly, no one seemed about to rush into their place. It looked as though they might be forced into going to Australia, where David could earn a living, though they wanted to stay in Britain and compete. Fortunately, Lucinda had already ridden one horse, Shannagh, for John Burbidge, who had built up his SR Direct Mail business into one of the biggest in Europe: although his main horse interest had been in show jumping, he was changing route – he rides in hunter trials himself – and early in 1983 came the announcement that he was sponsoring Lucinda and David.

And what a quick return he had, for Lucinda and Regal Realm, the World Champions, went to Badminton the firm favourites and utterly justified their status. As well as her record fifth win, Lucinda was fourth on another of the SR team, Beagle Bay; and if David had not had a spectacular but unlucky fall from Mairangi Bay at the Bull Pens, the Greens could well have had three in the top six. At the 1983 European Championships in Frauenfeld, Switzerland, she and Regal Realm got off to a moderate start, after some controversial dressage judging which placed them only twentieth, went marvellously well across country and clear show jumping to finish second to Rachel Bayliss on Mystic Minstrel. Omens for the future of the new sponsorship could hardly be better.

# Behind the Scenes at Frauenfeld, European Championships, 1983

Left: *A case of standing tall to check the plaits of Irish horse Santex*

Centre, above: *That sinking feeling – with the temperatures soaring, Lucinda Green tests the water in unorthodox style*

Centre, below: *Cooling off – Virginia Holgate's Night Cap*

Right, below: *Grease, liberally applied, protects the legs*

Right: *There is only one way to check a horse's temperature – Peter Scott-Dunn, the British team's vet, with Night Cap*

# 11
# Eventing in the Olympics

Los Angeles, 1984, will be one of the most important Olympic Games of all time for equestrian events, for it is there that an attempt must be made to retrieve the ground lost when most of the major equestrian nations of the free world boycotted the Moscow Games in 1980. Whatever the rights and wrongs of that boycott, and by now everyone who has thought about it all will have made up his or her own mind on that subject, there is little doubt that the schism which already existed was made just a little wider.

On the credit side, the claims against horse sport generally, and show jumping especially, of 'shamateurism' are now recognised as covering the whole gamut of international sport. The latest International Olympic Committee rules on eligibility, and the attitude of the Olympic authorities, indicate that they no longer seem to regard it as such a heinous crime, and although it may be a long time before the Olympic Games become 'open' to professionals as well as to professional-amateurs, those athletes who reach Olympian standard are rarely barred from pursuing their chosen sport full time.

Equestrian sport had a fairly inauspicious entrée into the Olympic movement: Count Clarence von Rosen, Master of the Horse to the King of Sweden, was fervently involved in trying to get horse sport included soon after the modern Olympic Games were restarted, in 1896, by Baron Pierre de Coubertin. When Count von Rosen suggested to the meeting of the International Olympic Committee in Athens, in 1906, that equestrian events, which had been part of the ancient Games,

should be revived, his proposals were rejected. The committee thought they would be too expensive – still an argument used today. But the Count had an ally in Baron de Coubertin, who asked him to prepare a detailed programme, with rules governing the sports, to be presented at the 1907 Congress of the IOC. The three competitions he suggested were dressage, a pentathlon and a game called *Jeu de Rose*, a sort of tag on horseback; this time the Congress looked with approval, and it was agreed that they should be included in the 1908 Games to be staged in London.

The main stadium for the Games was the White City, but this could not accommodate equestrian events, and Lord Lonsdale, the 'Yellow Earl', arranged to have them at his newly-instituted International Horse Show at Olympia; but at the last minute, he had to cry off, because his own show was so over-subscribed he and his committee did not think they could cope. Polo was included, however, and British teams finished first and second.

A full equestrian programme happened, finally, at the 1912 Games, most suitably, since these were held in Stockholm. The events were changed and were, in essence, the same as they are now: prize riding, now Grand Prix dressage; prize jumping (show jumping); and the military, a name which is still given to the three-day event in some parts of Europe, in particular in Germany. All the international equestrian events in those days were confined to Army officers, but the military was especially designed to test officers' chargers. It was in five phases, a long-distance ride of thirty-three miles, which included a separate three-mile cross-country, a steeplechase of two miles, show jumping and dressage. The latter ended the event, instead of starting it as it does now.

As if to pay tribute to Count von Rosen's persistence, all three team events, dressage, jumping and military, were won by Sweden, and the dressage and military individual golds went also to the host country. Lieutenant Axel Nordlander won the military on the British-bred Thoroughbred mare Lady Artist from a field of twenty-seven, from seven countries, of whom fifteen finished. The British, Danish and Belgian teams were all eliminated: two of the British riders in Stockholm, Colonel Paul Kenna, who rode in both the jumping and the event, and Lieutenant Colonel Bryan Lawrence, who fell and was concussed in the event, were both subsequent winners of the Victoria Cross. Germany, the United States and France were the other countries with teams, finishing in that order.

There was a long gap before the next Olympics while the world was embroiled in the horrors of the First World War, but the Swedish team, and Count Helmer Morner individually, triumphed at the resumption in Antwerp, 1920.

Only one man has ever won individual three-day-event gold medals at consecutive Olympics, the Dutchman Lieutenant Charles Ferdinand Pahud de Mortanges, of the Hussars, who had already been a member of the gold-medal team at the 1924 Games in Paris. He rode Marcroix to individual triumph in Amsterdam, 1928, where the event took on the precise formula used ever since, and in Los Angeles four years later. The expense of taking horses to Los Angeles during a period of world-wide recession resulted in extremely truncated fields: only fourteen riders, from five countries, took part in the event,

with just nine individual finishers and only two teams, the United States and the Netherlands.

No full teams completed the show jumping, so no team medals were awarded; and Lieutenant Clarence von Rosen, son of the man so largely responsible for the inclusion of the equestrian competitions, took bronze medals in both the event and the show jumping. Baron Takeichi Nishi won the jumping, the only Japanese ever to win an equestrian Olympic medal. He was twelfth in the three-day event at the Berlin Games in 1936, when Pahud de Mortanges, trying for his hat-trick, but on a different horse, was eliminated.

If the equestrian events in Los Angeles were thin, in Berlin they were perhaps the showpiece of an Olympics whose sole purpose, as far as the organisers were concerned, was to demonstrate to the world the supremacy of Nazi Germany. They could hardly have been more successful, for all three team gold medals and all three individual golds were won by Germans, and the three-day-event course was generally reckoned to have been

*Sweden's Axel Nordlander on Lady Artist, winners of the 'military' at the 1912 Olympics – a tribute to fellow Swede Count von Rosen's persistence in ensuring equestrian events were included in the Olympic Games*

*Ludwig Stubbendorf winning the 1936 Olympic Games in Berlin on Nurmi*

one of the most lethal ever. How different from the Munich Games of 1972 when the cross-country course was an object lesson in how to test horses, and riders, without horrific accidents or draining the animals to the limits of their endurance.

The fourth fence, in 1936, a post-and-rails into a pond, was the one that caused most of the damage: the pond was shown later to have been on false ground, and it was suggested that the home team knew the safe route through it. But that was never proved. Of the forty-six horses that attempted to jump it only eighteen did so unscathed; eighteen more fell, and another ten unseated their riders. Three horses were killed during the event, twenty-three of the fifty starters were eliminated and only four teams finished the course. Britain won her first equestrian Olympic medal, the team bronze, with ten teams failing to finish. It was a tale of disaster that made the recent events which have caused so much acrimonious discussion about cruelty look very tame indeed, and sickened many of those involved.

America's Earl Thompson, with his mare Jenny Camp, who had been the silver-medal winners in Los Angeles,

again filled the same position behind Ludwig Stubbendorf, on Nurmi.

It was twelve years, and another World War, before the Games were resumed, in London, 1948, when for the first time the British public was able to witness a sport which it has since adopted so enthusiastically. The three-day event was held at Aldershot, an appropriate choice for 'the military' since this is the headquarters of the British Army, but alas the home team was among the nine, out of fourteen starters, who failed to finish.

Major Peter Borwick, who finished seventeenth on the aptly-named Liberty, was the best placed of the British finishers, with Captain Bernard Chevallier on Aiglonne winning from the American Lieutenant Colonel Frank Henry on Swing Low; and the United States team won the gold for the first time. But perhaps the most significant result of the Aldershot event was that the Duke of Beaufort decided, after seeing it, that Britain should have a three-day event at which riders could gain the experience needed if they were to make their mark internationally. And Badminton, in his superb Gloucestershire parkland, began in 1949, destined to become the most important three-day event in the world.

Three-day eventing gradually built up its public,

*The dressage scene at the 1936 Berlin Olympics, a showcase for Hitler's Germany*

*Sweden's Hans von Blixen-Finecke, winner of the individual gold medal at Helsinki in 1952, on Jubal*

both in Britain and abroad, and became more international. The first European Championships were at Badminton in 1953 – when Major Lawrence Rook won on Starlight XV from Major Frank Weldon (the man later to run the event there for many years) with Kilbarry, and Britain was the only team to finish. Lawrence Rook's success was compensation for a sad mistake during the 1952 Olympics in Helsinki when, after a fall in which he was concussed, he insisted on remounting and finishing the course, but went the wrong side of a marker flag so that he and the team were eliminated. Even so they could not have beaten Sweden.

But even greater compensation was to come. The 1956 Olympic Games were held in Melbourne, but because of the Australian quarantine regulations, which are even more of a bar to inter-hemispherical competition than the distances involved, the equestrian events were staged on their own in Stockholm, and were an outstanding success. Protagonists of an equestrian Games

separate from the main body of Olympic competition – an increasing number since Moscow – habitually point to Stockholm, 1956, as a shining example.

If the British could be guaranteed a similar result, they would not take much persuading, for Weldon, Rook and Bertie Hill, a north Devon farmer who had been seventh in Helsinki, together won Britain's first equestrian gold medal, and Frank Weldon with Kilbarry took the individual bronze as well.

Britain went to Stockholm the reigning European Champions, and generally rated favourites: the same trio, plus Diana Mason on Tramella, had won the European title. Sheila Wilcox and High and Mighty might well have been in the Olympic side had women been allowed to ride in three-day events, but that was not permitted until Tokyo in 1964, and was the reason another of Britain's top women event riders, Anneli Drummond-Hay, with possibly the best horse ever, Merely-a-Monarch, turned from eventing to show jumping. Hill was riding Countryman III, a horse he had trained but which was now owned by the Queen, whose interest in the sport had been aroused.

Above: *Frank Weldon (left)
and Kilbarry, Bertie Hill on
Countryman III and Lawrence Rook
on Wild Venture, after winning the
team gold medal in Stockholm, 1956*

Left: *Petrus Kastenmann with
Illuster on his way to a gold medal
in Stockholm*

Right: *Golden time for Sweden in
Stockholm – Grand Prix dressage
winner Henri St Cyr (left)
congratulates Petrus Kastenmann,
the three-day event victor*

There were fifty-six riders from nineteen countries,
including, for the first time, a team from Australia.
Although they had brought horses with them from
Australia, all the horses they rode in the event had been
bought in England. The British led after the dressage,
but what had looked a reasonable cross-country course
when walked in sunshine turned into something of a
nightmare under a downpour of rain. Only Hill and
Countryman gained maximum bonus in the steeplechase,
and he had trouble going across country when he was
literally stuck on top of the twenty-second fence, a

Above: *Learning to swim in Stockholm – Frenchman Boughet and Ferney show how it should not be done*

Opposite above: *Italy's Molinari stands by in Stockholm as his unfortunate mount is helped off the Timber Rails. Thick mud didn't help matters*

Opposite below: *Russian hopes bite the dust in the Stockholm Olympics as Comrade Kouibyschev makes his exit during the show-jumping phase*

trakehner at the bottom of a steep gully; in the end Hill had to dismount and lead his horse to the top of the gully and start again. Even so they finished twelfth with Rook on Wild Venture sixth; both Wild Venture and Kilbarry had stops across country, but for which Kilbarry's bronze would have been a gold. This went to the Swede, Petrus Kastenmann, on Illuster.

Germany finished second and Canada third, their team including the evergreen Jim Elder, still a regular member of their show-jumping team, including that which won the 'Substitute Olympic' Rotterdam Festival in 1980.

Australian riders had had a taste of Olympic competition in Stockholm and came back in earnest for Rome: Brian Crago was the only survivor from the 1956 team, but his compatriots showed exactly what they could do at Badminton in the spring of 1960, when Bill Roycroft won on Our Solo, Laurie Morgan was second with Salad Days and Neale Lavis fourth on Mirrabooka. Anneli Drummond-Hay was best of the British, third on Perhaps, but women were still not eligible for the Olympic event.

Germany's final trial for Rome, at Luhmühlen, was

Above: *Denmark's Arne Preben Jensen just clears the notorious Concrete Pipes at the 1960 Rome Olympics*

Left: *Laurie Morgan of Australia, the individual gold-medal winner at the Rome Olympics, flanked by Switzerland's Anton Bühler (left), who won the bronze, and Australia's Neale Lavis who took the silver*

Opposite: *Even with a broken shoulder Australian Bill Roycroft puts on the style in Rome to help his country win the team gold medal in 1960*

interesting, too, for the top German rider (though second to a Dane) was Hans Günter Winkler, twice World Show Jumping Champion and winner of five Olympic show-jumping gold medals, who was reported as saying it was 'child's play' compared with international show jumping. Second German home then was Reiner Klimke, the current World Dressage Champion.

There have been many brave performances in the history of eventing, but few if any to surpass that of the Australians in Rome. The course was big enough, and badly built, with the worst fence number thirty-one, drainpipes jumped longways, with a 5-ft spread, that scraped, lamed and upset many horses. Lack of organisation had been apparent from the beginning, when the dressage judges, with no whistle or bell, had to clap to bring riders into the arena, and shout at them if they made an error of course. Sweden, USSR and Germany were leading after the dressage, but all were eliminated across country, during which the Australians, who had been sixth, swept into the lead.

At halfway in the cross-country Bill Roycroft and Our Solo led, even though they had fallen at the drainpipes and Bill was in hospital with a broken shoulder. Switzerland's Hans Schwarzenbach, on Burn Trout, took over the lead, to be passed by Neale Lavis on Mirrabooka; then Brian Crago and Sabre went ahead, but Sabre broke down in the process. Finally Laurie

*Frenchman Jack Le Goff, seen here at the Rome Olympics on Image, went on to become the American team's trainer and chef d'équipe*

*On the way to a soaking, Canada's Thomas Gayford on Pepper Knowes at the Rome Olympics, 1960*

Morgan and Salad Days became the fourth Australian to head the placings, and stayed there. Australia was well ahead with the show jumping to come, but Sabre was out, and Roycroft in hospital. The tough Australian, whose frequent visits to Britain since have been so popular, took himself to the Piazza di Siena, and rode Our Solo clear in the jumping; Mirrabooka was clear too and although Salad Days had a fence down and time faults he easily took the individual gold, with Lavis second, and clinched the team gold.

Switzerland's Anton Bühler won the bronze, with his team second and France third. Britain, who had had horse problems, came in fourth, as did Michael Bullen, riding Cottage Romance, a fine performance considering that Michael, whose sister Jane went on to take a team gold in Mexico, had ridden in his first three-day event only the previous season, when going *hors concours* in the European Championships at Harewood.

Few event horses had, or have since, flown as far as those for the Tokyo Games in 1964, and the journey may well have cost the United States a team gold, for Michael Plumb's experienced horse Markham panicked so badly he had to be put down on the flight. Plumb then teamed up with Bold Minstrel, who arrived only ten days before the event, yet his side still took the silver behind Italy, whose Mauro Checcoli and Surbean showed the necessity of being absolutely fit for such an occasion. The site, some eighty miles from Tokyo at the foot of a volcano, was set on lava which produced patchy going. Only twelve teams started, seven fewer than in Rome, with the Australians favourites both on form and because they had had a shorter journey; but they never looked like repeating their Roman gold performance, finally finishing seventh.

Women were, at last, allowed to take part, and the honour of being the first to do so fell to the American Lana Dupont, on Mister Wister, who finished thirty-third and had the discard score in the US team. Richard Meade made his Olympic debut for Britain, but what could have been a glorious beginning went sour: he and Barberry were ahead, by only just over a point, going into the show jumping, but had three fences down, and six time penalties, and dropped to eighth place, one ahead of Ben Jones on Master Bernard. Mike Bullen, after a fall on the chase and another on the cross-country with Sea Breeze, was eliminated, as was James Templer and M'Lord Connolly, and the British team.

Four years later Meade rode one of the greatest horses to go eventing, Cornishman V, who, in finishing fourth in Mexico helped Britain win the team gold, and in Munich made history with another team gold, and his owner's daughter, Mary Gordon-Watson, in the saddle. Rain had fallen throughout speed and endurance day in Tokyo, and sheeted down at Avandaro, Mexico, turning a fairly innocuous river into a raging torrent. Jane Bullen and her tiny Badminton winner Our Nobby twice fell after jumping it – his feet sticking in the deep mud – and Derek Allhusen collected twenty penalties when he could not turn Lochinvar sharply enough at the second fence. But Allhusen still ended the day in fourth place, with Richard Meade on Cornishman and Ben Jones with The Poacher close up, and the British team in the lead. But for their falls Jane and Our Nobby would have led also: the rain increased in intensity and when Meade rode it was almost impossible to see some of the fences, let alone jump them.

Despite the rigours of the cross-country, the show jumping played an enormous part in the result. Jimmy Wofford of the USA and Kilkenny were certain of a medal, probably silver, until Kilkenny slipped up on the flat; and when Frenchman Jean-Jacques Guyon with Pitou had a fence down the Soviet rider Pavel Deev had a winning chance on Paket – but jumped the wrong fence and was eliminated, and with him his team. So Guyon was left with the gold, Derek Allhusen and Lochinvar took the silver and the bronze went to Michael Page on Foster for the United States, who were runners-up to Britain for the team medals. Meade on Cornishman and Jones on The Poacher finished fourth and fifth and Jane with Our Nobby eighteenth.

British eventing went through a golden streak at this time, victories including the 1970 World Championships, when Mary Gordon-Watson and Cornishman V won the individual title ahead of Richard Meade on The Poacher – only Britain and France survived a horrendous cross-country course at Punchestown – and the European Championships of 1969 and 1971, with Mary on Cornishman and Princess Anne with Doublet taking the individual golds. The Munich Olympics set the seal in a most magnificent way, with the team retaining their gold medal, and Richard Meade becoming the first British rider to win an individual gold in an Olympic three-day event, on Derek Allhusen's home-bred Laurieston.

Munich was a model for international events. The equestrian events were based at Riem, about ten miles outside the Bavarian capital, in a £5 million complex

*Major Derek Allhusen, Jane Bullen, Richard Meade and Sergeant Ben Jones after winning the team gold medal in the 1968 Mexico Olympics*

*Jane Bullen, winner of a team gold medal for Britain in the 1968 Mexico Olympics, on the great Our Nobby*

that provided horses and grooms with splendid accommodation and training grounds, and a superb stadium for the dressage and jumping. The cross-country course was so fair that twelve of the eighteen teams and forty-eight of the seventy-three riders finished the event, but still it asked enough questions to give the best horses and riders the greatest chance of winning. To the delight of the crowd Horst Karsten and Sioux led the dressage but they, and five of the top six in the dressage, failed to complete the cross-country: Jan Jonsson, from Sweden, on Sarajevo, who eventually took the bronze medal, was the sole exception.

Laurieston, at peak fitness ready for the speed and endurance, was a little way down the list, but only just over seventeen points behind the leader. Britain had had to make a last-minute change to their team when Debbie West's Baccarat, runner-up in the 1971 European Championships, went lame. Bridget Parker was brought in on Cornish Gold, to join Meade on Laurieston, Mary Gordon-Watson with Cornishman and Mark Phillips on Great Ovation.

Fences twenty-two and twenty-three were the most crucial, a bank followed by a post and rails, and Cornishman, leading the way and jumping what turned out to be the 'wrong' side, had a stop there which cost him a bronze medal. Jonsson and Sarajevo went fast and clear to overtake them, and Mrs Parker with Cornish Gold consolidated the British position, also round with just one stop. But Great Ovation, who had looked fairly 'dead' in the dressage, had a disaster of a round, with a fall at the fourth fence and a second fall and two refusals before finishing the course. This put all the pressure on Meade, but he lived up to it in the way we have come to expect, fast, clear and into the lead. Italy's Alessandro Argenton on Woodland, third last to go, climbed into second place, but had to be satisfied with the silver when all the top four went clear in the show jumping.

For the third Olympics in succession the United States team was second, but they came good with a vengeance in Montreal, when Tad Coffin and Mike Plumb filled the top two individual places for them also. The equestrian events were based at Bromont, some forty miles south of Montreal and not far from the US border, under a shadow of strict, and increasing, security, carried sometimes to absurd lengths. Jack Le Goff, former French Olympic rider, took over as trainer to the US event team in 1971 and did for them what Bert de Nemethy did for the American show jumpers, welding them into an elegant and effective force.

Germany's Karl Schultz, with Madrigal, led the dressage, with the US just ahead of his side on a team basis, and Britain third. Lucinda Prior-Palmer and Be Fair, the European Champions, were fifth, but disaster struck this brilliant chestnut on the cross-country; near the finish he slipped a ligament from his hock – just as Columbus had done when he and Mark Phillips looked likely to win the 1974 World Championship – and was so lame he never ran in a three-day event again. The course was run on a golf course, hilly, with well-built fences and a tricky water complex. Hugh Thomas' Playamar came down there, broke down and, with him and Be Fair out, the British team was finished, even though Richard Meade gave Jacob Jones a brilliant ride into fourth place.

As in Tokyo and Mexico, cross-country day brought a torrential rainstorm, so that the sandy steeplechase course rode very dead, and much of the rest of the course became waterlogged or slippery. Otto Ammermann, third on Volturno in the dressage, missed his way on the chase course, went back after warning shouts and was later disqualified for 'outside assistance'. Bruce Davidson, winner of the World Championship in 1974 and 1978 – the only rider to have won the title twice – lost his chance of adding an individual Olympic gold with a fall at one of the water fences.

*Nearly there – Richard Meade powers on with Laurieston at the Munich Olympics in 1972. They went on to win the individual gold and a team gold medal*

Five of the eleven teams were eliminated, and at the end of the second phase Schultz and Madrigal maintained their lead, with Coffin on Ballycor second and Plumb with the seven-year-old Better and Better third. But Schultz and Madrigal hit two show-jumping fences to let the Americans up above him on the podium, as they were in the final team placings.

Bill Roycroft, hero of Rome, was again in the

*Everything must be in order – Captain Mark Phillips putting the finishing touches to Princess Anne's topper before her dressage test in Montreal*

Australian quartet, together with one of his sons, Wayne, who rode Laurenson into fifth, and their team took the bronze.

After the Russian invasion of Afghanistan most of the major equestrian nations boycotted the Moscow Games, holding their own 'Festivals' instead: only three non-Iron Curtain countries, Italy, Mexico and India, competed in the Moscow event, which the Soviet team

won by a convincing margin from Italy. They had three of the top four, but the individual gold went to Federico Euro Roman, on Rossinan. At the Fontainebleau Festival Denmark's Nils Haagensen proved his 1981 European Championship success was no fluke by repeating it, on Monaco. A former Olympic dressage rider, Haagensen won his European title only some eighteen months after taking up eventing, but Monaco retired after Fontainebleau and he is still looking for a horse of similar calibre.

Jose Ortelli, of the Argentine, whose horse Bravio died at Fontainebleau, was suspended by the FEI for cruelty – originally for two years, later reduced to one – and the Argentine *chef d'équipe* was also suspended. Public concern has been very vociferous about the demands made in three-day events, and the authorities are wise to heed it. After the mishaps of Lexington one can only hope Los Angeles, 1984, will have no such problems to face.

Compared with Los Angeles, 1932, when a total of only thirty-two riders from six countries took part – three Swedish riders competed in both the three-day event and the show jumping, including Clarence von Rosen who won a bronze medal in each – the Games to be held there fifty-two years later look sure to have bumper fields, with more than thirty countries likely to be represented in the show jumping alone, just under thirty in the event and over twenty in the dressage.

Headquarters for the equestrian events is to be Santa Anita Park, one of the most attractive racecourses in the United States, with facilities for the horses, riders and grooms, and spectators, that can confidently be expected to prove as good as at any previous Olympic Games, and a great deal better than most. Those of us who remember the car-parking chaos at Bromont, scene of the equestrian competitions for the Montreal Games, will especially welcome the fact that Santa Anita has 130 acres of hard-surfaced car parks, big enough to hold 22,000 cars.

There is stabling for 2100 horses, in fifty-five barns, an equine hospital, with facilities – that one hopes will not be needed – for surgery, and of course a horse ambulance, and living quarters for more than 600 people. The grooms' quarters in Munich were exemplary, but they should have little to complain about in Los Angeles either.

*Nearly down, but not out, Germany's Karl Schultz and Madrigal blunder at Bromont*

Above: *Germany's Otto Ammerman is hardly visible as he parts company with Volturno at the Serpent fence in the 1978 World Championships in Lexington*

Opposite above: *The impressive main entrance to Santa Anita Park, venue of the equestrian events at the 1984 Olympic Games*

Opposite below: *The stable area at Santa Anita designed to accommodate 2100 horses – plenty of room for the 1984 Olympians*

Santa Anita, which opened in 1934, has racing for nearly ninety days a year, from December until April, and a huge grandstand, but special stands more suitable for show jumping and dressage events will be erected for the Games, for between 35,000 and 45,000 people. With the exception of the speed and endurance phase of the horse trials, all the equestrian events will be held there – even the final show jumping, which is normally held, just prior to the closing ceremony, in the main Olympic arena of whichever city is hosting the Games. This could not happen in Los Angeles, apparently, because preparations for the closing ceremony are scheduled to take four hours, and that would mean the show jumping being finished by 11.00 a.m. It would have to start at around 6.00 a.m., when there would not be an enormous audience anyway, so the decision was to have it, too, at Santa Anita. It was in many ways regrettable, even if almost inevitable, since this is show jumping's biggest shop window to the general public.

The other major choice the FEI had to make was where to hold the event's speed and endurance phase. Weather conditions in Los Angeles, liable to be hot and humid and maybe with smog, ruled out the city itself, for no one wanted a repetition of the disasters of the World Championships at Lexington, Kentucky, which were also run in hot, humid weather. After much searching, Fairbanks Ranch, at Rancho Santa Fe, thirty miles north of San Diego and only two miles from the Pacific Ocean, was chosen: it has low humidity and a permanent breeze from the ocean.

It is a two-hour drive from Los Angeles, where the dressage and show-jumping phases are to be held, so there will be rest days between each of the three phases, elongating the three-day event into one lasting six days.

Neil Ayer, one of the most experienced men in American eventing, was chosen to design the cross-country course, and there is no doubt his is a formidable task, for it is being built entirely artificially, in conjunction with a golf course that will be used after the Olympic Games. Nearly two million cubic yards of earth will have been excavated and landscaped, and then grassed; it is very sandy soil, so that it may not be a great tragedy if the grass is patchy, but as it grows all the year round Mr Ayer is expecting a good cover. 'It is a big job, but everyone is determined to have it done well, and on time,' Mr Ayer said last year.

He is planning his course in close liaison with the architect for the golf course, Theodore Robinson, and one great benefit for spectators will be that the fences are quite closely grouped. With typical American know-how they have even diverted a river from its original bed.

In Montreal the speed and endurance day of the three-day event produced the largest single crowd at any of the competitions: how Los Angeles will compare is a matter for conjecture, but with the city of San Diego so close – in addition to those who make the journey from Los Angeles – the 1984 Olympic three-day event could put the sport on the North American map to an extent that the World Championships in Lexington, Kentucky, never quite managed.

# 12
# The Other Side of Eventing

No one would deny that eventing is one of the toughest of equestrian sports, but there have been times in the past when people have had good cause to question the fairness of some of the courses and the reasoning of certain riders.

Because eventing is so demanding, there is a very thin dividing line between being tough and downright hard – some people might even go as far as to say cruel. But that is too strong a word – of all the riders I have met while writing about the sport in all corners of the world, I have yet to find one who did not care deeply about his or her horses.

Of course there have been times when, in the excitement of the moment, riders have been downright stupid, or uncaring; others, not wishing to let down their team or themselves, have done things they have since regretted; but, on the whole, all connected with the horses have had the animals' welfare at heart. That is how it must be if equestrian sport is to endure.

Those who have made serious mistakes have paid dearly, spending time suspended by the FEI (and therefore unable to compete) or being pilloried in the newspapers and magazines. And that, too, is how it should be, because nobody in their right mind wants to see horses deliberately being asked too many questions or being hurt for the benefit of any individual or nation.

The ultimate decisions must come from the FEI, the sport's ruling body, and if, in the future, riders are too hard on their mounts, causing them to be hurt through sheer incompetence, then those in command must crack down even harder. They must not permit a few thoughtless riders to ruin a perfectly good sport either for the public or for the great majority of riders who genuinely do care.

Sometimes, of course, it is not the riders themselves who are to blame; they cannot help it if a course or particular fence is too testing. On such occasions the responsibility must be placed firmly with the course builder, or the technical delegate. They, too, have their responsibilities, and must be prepared to stand up and be counted – it cannot be a one-sided situation, with the riders taking all the blame.

Anyone who visited Kiev for the 1973 European Championships would have surely been forgiven for asking what on earth fence two was doing on the course at all.

Fence two was a wide parallel set over a deep ditch, with one of the most difficult approaches I have ever seen. In the views of many people it should not have come so early on in the competition and it was to take a heavy toll. Even those reporters who did not know very much about horses – many were sent to Kiev simply to cover Princess Anne's participation in the Championships – stood nearby to watch how riders would cope with it.

As the competition progressed horses and riders tumbled down at that obstacle like skittles in a bowling alley; one of those to bite the dust there was the Princess herself who, riding Goodwill, was defending the title she had won on Doublet at Burghley in 1971. She took a bad bruising and wisely decided not to subject her horse to further punishment.

*All looked well for Princess Anne and Goodwill as they negotiated the dreaded fence two at Kiev in 1973 . . . but they hit the ground hard on landing and were lucky to escape serious injury*

At the end of the day there had been twenty falls and fifteen eliminations at that particular fence: clearly someone had made a dreadful error.

The rest of the course had, for the majority of competitors, ridden fairly well in comparison, yet that one fence marred the whole event. Some horses fell, became stuck fast in the gully and had to be helped out by officials. It was not a pleasant sight and should not have happened. The big question is, why did those in authority allow the fence to be passed in the first place?

Some people might suggest that the fault lay not with the fence, but with the calibre of horses taking part in those Championships. But that argument simply does not stand up: for twenty horses from thirty-six starters to come down at one fence must indicate that something was very wrong with it, or with its position on the course. No obstacle should be responsible for such a huge number of falls, no matter how important the event.

There have been other unfortunate instances at courses in other countries, too, notably at Fontainebleau during the 1980 substitute Olympics, when an Argentinian rider asked his horse too many questions, the exhausted animal broke a leg and then had to be destroyed. There must be no room in eventing for that sort of behaviour, and the rider in question was later, quite rightly, suspended. The horse must come first and if anyone thinks differently then they would do well to leave the sport.

There have been suggestions in the past that the team events should be taken out of the three-day event, and that riders should compete in the championships only as individuals. But it is not something which would meet with much approval among the British riders, because with them it is the team effort that counts; any personal glory is good but purely incidental – a worthy ideal.

However, it has been pointed out that, if one is not riding for a team, a lot of the pressure to complete the course at all costs is removed; if an individual wants to pull out, he or she can do so without destroying the team effort.

A typical example of what a rider has to go through to enable a team to finish, and perhaps win a medal, came at that event in Kiev, and concerned the brilliant and very brave Janet Hodgson. She took two very bad

falls and yet climbed back into the saddle, despite injuries which many men may not have withstood, and finished the event in glory. She was hurt but she wanted to carry on for the team. It was a truly magnificent effort and so impressed the Russians that they presented her with a special prize for bravery.

By proving that she could take a great deal of punishment and see the event through to the end, Janet also helped to destroy the arrogant theory that women cannot stand up to injuries as well as men.

But if the same thing had happened to someone riding as an individual, would they have put themselves at so much risk, and endured as much pain as Janet did? Only those involved at the time can truly know the answer to that question – but it is one worth thinking about.

The fact remains that massive, awkward fences such

as that at Kiev, and another notorious obstacle made up of concrete pipes at the Rome Olympics in 1960, are simply not essential to good sport. Nor are those courses which are too long and demanding, so that when a horse finishes – if indeed he is lucky enough to do so – his tongue is hanging out with fatigue. There is no need to subject horses to such an ordeal – no matter how easy the event is, there will always be a result, so why make it so terribly difficult? Horse trials comprise three disciplines – dressage, cross-country and show jumping – all three are important and if everything is properly balanced an event can be enjoyed by all.

There is also a case for those in command to ask themselves if the qualifying system should be revised. What might be considered an adequate pre-championship test in one country might be absolutely lamentable when compared with that in another. It is all a question of standards and, as has been proved over and over again throughout sporting history, some standards are higher than others. It is up to those in charge of the sport as a whole to make sure that high qualifying standards for major championships are complied with everywhere.

If they are not, there is the likelihood of some countries always overfacing their mounts in international competitions simply because their horses are not able to cope with big fences and long courses against top opposition. Such animals should not be in the event in the first place.

Of course, people want to compete, if only for the honour of representing their country. That is perfectly understandable. But it most certainly does not make it right for them to overface their horses. Those whose capabilities at top international level might be considered questionable must permit people with more experience to make the right decision for them – and, more importantly, for their horses, because it is they who invariably suffer in the final analysis.

The big question is how far should we go in the name of equestrian sport? For example, when the World Championships took place in Lexington the combination of humidity, and some difficult fences, exhausted some of the horses and there were those who had to be given oxygen afterwards.

Certainly veterinary treatment in such cases is of comfort to the horses, but surely there are two points to be made: first, why were the Championships staged at that particular time of year instead of later, when the

weather might have been better; and second, if a horse is in such a bad condition that he requires oxygen, is it right to have asked him to go that far and, indeed, to expect him to carry on in the event thereafter?

There will be those who answer that too much fuss is being made and that, as the horses used for eventing are sporting horses, it is up to the riders to make the decisions. To a point that is correct, but there must come a time when other opinions count, particularly when those on the sidelines, who have no vested interests, consider that horses are being asked too much. It is a matter of opinion but a serious enough one for debate.

Of course, eventing is hard and has always been so, but that is not a valid excuse because it must all come down to a matter of degree, and how far it is wise to go when using horses for sport.

After all, if a horse is pushed so hard that he is suffering merely because the rider concerned wants to win above all else, that must be totally wrong. It is up to the rider to know just what the horse is capable of doing, and to keep within those limits. Otherwise the whole thing becomes absurd and dangerous for all involved.

All is not gloom, however, and there have been times when a rider has wisely pulled out. As, for instance, that famous occasion in the World Championships at Burghley in 1974, when Captain Mark Phillips held a commanding lead after the cross-country section but his horse, Columbus, slipped a ligament off his hock and was withdrawn. Asked afterwards how he felt about losing a title that had seemed his for the asking, he replied, 'There was no question of going on – the horse was injured.'

That, in fact, is what it is all about and Phillips showed what a true sportsman he is by accepting the situation with good grace. He did not show anger – he just put his mount first and the horse recovered, eventually, to compete again.

Courses in Britain are fair, although some are designed to make the riders think and quite often alternative routes are made available. Burghley, in particular, has always produced good, fair courses and, although there are always the inevitable falls, the horses who compete there are never asked too many searching questions. When asked one year what sort of course was to be expected at Burghley Charles Stratton, who runs the event, said, 'We do not build courses to kill horses.'

That comment was made after the press had been carrying stories about the number of horses who were being pushed too hard abroad, over courses that were fairly stiff. The sport was, at the time, going through a bad patch, and reporters and public alike were keeping a very close watch on it.

*How not to ride eventing: Argentinian Fernando Zuviria and his mount Ucase taking a heavy fall at Fontainebleau, 1980*

There is no denying that a tough, rugged course of enormous obstacles leads to an exciting competition, with plenty of falls and drama – in other words a spectacle. But it can all too easily lead to heartache.

Because there is always a very real element of danger every time a horse takes off to negotiate a fence, it is only logical to make it as safe as possible. There will still be thrills and spills, but with any luck they will not end on a serious note. Eventing is a great sport: it would be ridiculous to destroy it trying to be too clever.

*The Serpent at Lexington has a lot to answer for . . . Australia's Peter Byrne (Peerless Don) makes a dramatic exit there (above left) . . . Holland's Alice Waanders and Regal Abbot crash on landing (above top) . . . and America's Ralph Hill on Sergeant Gilbert is down and nearly out (above) . . . the World Championships, 1978*

# 13
# A Princess in Sport

Britain is exceptionally lucky in having a member of the Royal family who plays a very active role in eventing, for by merely taking part Princess Anne has helped to put the sport on the map – and into the pages of practically every national newspaper both in Britain and abroad.

But her participation has not been as a rider who merely plays at the sport. Her story is one of total dedication, which led to victory in the individual European Championship at Burghley in 1971, when she rode Doublet, and to her receiving the Sportswoman of the Year award.

It would have been all too simple for the Princess to have gone out for an easy time in eventing, riding at the occasional show, and not risking the hurly burly of top-class horse trials, where even the slightest mistake can lead to injury to both rider and mount. That, however, is not her style and she proved beyond any doubt that she could not only ride, but also had an abundance of courage.

It is also prudent to point out that on many occasions Princess Anne has really had it harder than many other riders, because her every move, in and out of the saddle, was and still is recorded by hundreds of eager photographers trying, with all their highly professional skills, to get the best pictures of her. It is their job to try hard, that is what they are paid for, but sometimes it can be distracting for a rider.

It highlights the pressure the Princess takes at events up and down the country, and when one remembers that a major part of eventing is dressage, where even the slightest noise or movement can play havoc with even the calmest horse's nerves, it is easy to see why total concentration is so very necessary.

*Right in focus – Princess Anne takes a well-earned rest after riding across country*

*Princess Anne and Goodwill in harmony at dressage – one false move can destroy a test. The 1976 Olympic Games at Montreal*

*High-flying Doublet gives the water a clear berth at Badminton*

Apart from photographers and reporters, the public, too, turn up in their hundreds of thousands at major events such as Badminton. They are, of course, interested in everything that is going on, but it can be guaranteed that the moment Princess Anne climbs into the saddle all eyes are turned to her. It is human nature: the public loves having a sporting Princess and, naturally, wants to see everything she does. But it all adds to the pressure and it is truly remarkable how calm she manages to remain when faced with a formidable course across country, or riding a horse in the dressage arena. It is

certainly not easy, but over the years she has stood up to everything and come through with flying colours. Royal training helps – but there is also a lot of personal effort.

To be a three-day-event rider a person must have, apart from a suitable horse, or horses, several important attributes, particularly if he or she wants to take on and beat the best in the world. Two of those attributes must be skill and bravery; without them there is no way the rider will make it to the top.

Being a member of the Royal family does not give Princess Anne any special immunity where injury is concerned. That was amply demonstrated in 1973 when she went to the Ukraine to defend her European title, riding Goodwill, and met up with the now notorious second fence which caused havoc, not only to her, but to many other competitors as well. She hit the ground hard that day, was badly bruised and was lucky not to have finished up with far more serious injuries. At a time like that it is right for any rider to want to go away quietly and nurse any wounds.

In Princess Anne's case, with the fall went the European title, which was a double blow for her. But that did not stop many of the foreign press descending upon her like locusts on a wheat field. Of course, they had a right to want to get the best photograph, or quote, but it was a classic example of what she has to put up with and many people thought she should have been left alone.

It must be made clear, however, that she really did take it all with great fortitude; it cannot be easy, or indeed much fun, to hit the ground at nearly thirty miles an hour.

After winning the coveted European title, and then losing it in the dust of the Ukraine, the Princess might have been forgiven for calling it a day. After all, she had achieved what some riders spend a lifetime seeking, and was there any real reason for going on and risking life and limb? Indeed, what was left?

The answer was the Olympics, the greatest of all sporting challenges; she was selected for the Montreal Games and became the first member of the Royal family to ride in any Games. Even to get there was a great personal achievement and a time of pride for the nation.

Unfortunately, it was not to have a fairytale end because she fell with Goodwill, though she remounted to finish. To do so over that particular course was an achievement in itself.

That incident, although probably extremely disappointing for the Princess, proved to anyone foolish enough to believe she did not have what it takes that they were wrong. No one competes in the Olympics, at any sport, unless they are very good at what they do. Of course, to win a gold medal is a wonderful achievement, but what really matters is taking part, and being good enough to do so.

When one considers that the Royal family's history is steeped in a tradition of riding, it is not surprising that Princess Anne decided to ride horses in competition. That she reached the top was a natural, but by no means easy progression for her. She gives the impression that once she has made up her mind to do something, it gets done. And that does not only concern her equestrian career.

It must also be remembered that she has not been given any preferential treatment as a rider merely because she happens to be the daughter of the Queen. She most certainly would not want it that way, and anything she has got out of the sport has been by her own efforts and talent.

When the Princess first broke through to top-flight eventing she made it clear that she wanted 'to be treated like any other sportswoman' and that is how it has been ever since, even though, on occasions, security has, rightly, taken precedence. For those who travel the world with her, that is readily understood.

But during her years of creating sporting headlines and, by so doing, promoting eventing, she has never once refused to answer any sensible question about her horses or her riding activities.

It is lucky, perhaps, that both the Princess, and her husband, Captain Mark Phillips, share the same interests

*Princess Anne deep in thought after a Badminton briefing in the Memorial Hall*

and both love horses and eventing. But, whereas Captain Phillips needs to be sponsored, which he is by Range Rover, Princess Anne has to spend her own money on her horses and equipment.

In 1983 it was announced that Captain Phillips had built his own course at their home in Gatcombe Park at Minchinhampton, Gloucestershire, in order to stage an event there. The land on the estate at Gatcombe is ideal for an eventing course, and much of the material for the fences came from the surrounding area. It was also fitting that Phillips designed the course himself; he has had a wealth of experience and knows exactly what is required. Princess Anne was always on hand to give

*Not so Luckington Lane! Mark Phillips steps out of the way as Columbus turns a somersault at Badminton*

*What goes up, must come down. Nicola McIrvine at the Gatcombe Trials, parting company with The Knave*

*That's the way – Captain Mark Phillips with Michael Bullen and Jim Gilmore (in the background) at Gatcombe in 1983*

*Watch out! Mark Phillips on Classic Lines hits the second element of the Pigsty at Badminton, takes a crashing fall and rolls away. 'What on earth was that all about!' he seems to ask his horse*

*A classic style – Princess Anne on Purple Star, her first event horse*

valuable help and advice and that is why they are successful, because they work as a team.

Captain Phillips had won a gold medal in the Olympic squad in 1972 at Munich and although the Princess had also been short-listed for those Games, her mount Doublet had leg trouble and was withdrawn. Two years later, however, she rode Goodwill, to finish twelfth in the World Championships.

In 1975, at Luhmühlen, in West Germany, the Princess went close to winning the European Championship again, this time with Goodwill. The only anxious moment, as far as the public was concerned, came when her mount stood right off at the Boat, on the cross-country course, but he took it all in his stride and galloped on bravely to the finish, gaining his rider an individual silver, and one for the team as well.

The individual winner that year was Lucinda Prior-Palmer (now Mrs Green) on Be Fair, who was later to go on to even greater heights and win the individual World title, at the same venue, but on the Australian-bred Regal Realm.

Princess Anne, however, did have the satisfaction of finishing in front of the Russian, Peter Gornuschko, who rode Gusar to win the individual bronze and a team gold medal. After her experiences in Kiev, many thought that finishing ahead of a Russian was justice indeed for the Princess!

In 1977 she did not compete at all because her first child, Peter, was born, and some people considered that this happy event might herald the end of her competitive career. That, however, was far from the case, and even after her daughter, Zara, was born, it was not long before Her Royal Highness was in the saddle once again.

During the 1983 season she had to rely on novices, after Stevie B, the horse everyone thought might take her back to the top, was sold. But, with a little luck in finding the right mount, the Princess could most certainly be right in the firing line once again. It may even be that one of her young horses will come good. Without trying, the Princess can add thousands of people to the gate of any event, and organisers all over the country must be delighted when they see her horses entered. She did say, however, in 1983, that she would not be riding three-day eventing in the foreseeable future.

To reach the top a rider must concentrate, travel a great deal and compete in many classes that never rate a mention in the press – and be prepared to take the good times with the bad. It is not all Badmintons and Burghleys and European or World Championships and, in this respect, Princess Anne is no different from anyone else. That hard work must be done.

But her life is not given solely to competing, because her civil duties take up a great deal of her time, and she must fit in her sporting career the best way she can. If her official duties require her to travel abroad for long periods then she has to go and everything else must be pushed into the background. At times it must be very hard for her to cope, but she manages admirably.

Apart from her participation in eventing, the Princess also goes out of her way to help others, particularly the Riding for the Disabled Organisation of which she is Patron. She spends a good deal of time dashing from one end of the country to the other to attend functions and give much-needed encouragement to the disabled. What she has to say to them must be highly beneficial since she knows from personal experience the pleasures to be had from riding horses and ponies. There must be many occasions when her timetable is thrown into confusion because she regularly stays longer with RDA groups than is originally planned.

The Princess also knows that there are many, many people who give their time freely to handicapped riders,

either leading their ponies, or helping them both in and out of the saddle. She makes a point of giving them every encouragement, too. That is why she is a great success at both equestrian sport and official duties – because she genuinely cares.

*Out in the cold – in the weather, that is. Princess Anne on Soul Song at Gatcombe Park, 1982*

No matter what else happens during her sporting career, her name is in the record books for all time, not only as a Princess who took part in the tough sport of horse trials but as a lady who went out, tackled the best, and won a European Championship. Not many people have achieved that.

# 14
# David Green
# ~A Profile

David Green, husband of World Champion Lucinda and, like her, part of the SR Direct Mail team, did not start riding until he was sixteen, and 'hated it at first. The first time I sat on a horse, before it even had time to walk away, I jumped off. The feeling of sitting up there without any control – I just hated it. But I've always loved horses, so I had to make myself like riding.'

David, who now has British nationality, was born in Australia, which has a great tradition of success in international three-day events, usually through unconventional methods, and David Green's way was to ride every day for two years without a saddle. 'I rode everywhere bareback, and got confidence more and more each day.' Not that this was entirely of his own choosing: 'I had the pony, but no saddle, and a saddle cost about 400 dollars. So I didn't have much choice!'

He was given his first pony when his parents bought a place with some acreage just outside Brisbane. His family were not at all 'horsey', and all his early instruction came from the Pony Club. 'That was what got me eventing. Our Pony Club chief instructor had just come back from England, where he had been on holiday. He went to Badminton, and was eventing mad: otherwise I might have done show jumping.'

David's method of getting to like riding, and incidentally producing a secure seat that has proved indispensable – though even this could not keep him in Mairangi Bay's saddle at Badminton, 1983, when the Bull Pens produced one of the most spectacular unseatings for many a year – very quickly bore fruit. 'I was a late starter,' says David, but within a couple of years he was on the Australian short-list for the Moscow Olympics. In the end the Australian Equestrian Federation, like those of most other countries, boycotted the Moscow Games, but it led to his meeting Lucinda.

'I was on the list to come over for the Games, and the selectors wanted me to ride another horse in the Melbourne event. The horse was in Sydney, a thousand miles away, and I drove down one weekend to try him. He belonged to some friends so I stayed with them – I wasn't even going that weekend, but I changed my mind and went – and when I got there they told me there was a lecture that evening, and would I like to go. I said yes, though we did not even know who was giving it. Just someone from England – some Pom! It was Lucinda.'

After the lecture they were talking, about the proposed boycott among other things. 'I said that I had some good horses and I did not want to waste them when they were at the stage to do something big. So I thought of bringing them to England, and did she know where I could stay in England? She said I could stay here.' 'Here' is Lucinda's lovely family house at Appleshaw, near Andover in Hampshire, where the couple now keep their strong team of international and up-and-coming horses. They married in December 1981.

The success that Australian riders have had in the

---

*Splashing his way to success, David and Mairangi Bay winning the first ever Gatcombe Trials in 1983*

northern hemisphere is all the more surprising considering the problems they have at home, and the much smaller number of riders who take part in the sport. Distance is of course the major problem, and just as David thought nothing of driving a thousand miles to try out a horse, so they will travel just as far, and farther, to compete in an event. 'There are one-day trials every weekend, if you're prepared to travel. And normally four three-day events a year, at Sydney, Melbourne, Adelaide and Perth, but they've just started a new one at Brisbane.'

The season is a winter one, from March to September. 'There are no events in the summer, it would be much too hot. In Queensland horses will have a sweat on at six o'clock in the morning just standing in the paddock, and often you have to go and hose them down during the day.'

They do not have nearly as many top horses as in Britain. 'In an advanced class a good entry would be about twenty. Though you might get sixty or seventy in a combined novice and intermediate.'

Australia walked away with the team gold medal, and individual gold and silver, in the Rome Olympics in 1960, in a heroic display that still rings proudly in the annals of eventing; but although recent ventures have not been so successful, they have not been too far away.

'We were fourth in Munich, third in Montreal, third in Fontainebleau – we've always still been there. But Australian dressage is bloody awful. Still the courses at home are very big, really good preparation for any international event. I think if you put the eighty or so riders who went round Badminton this year into an Australian event, you'd have fewer clear rounds than you did at Badminton,' says David.

'A lot of the courses are very big, very spindly and badly-built. Then the horses come over here, and they think it's Christmas! Lovely big, well-built fences, and they just go.'

Living in England is 'marvellous. As long as I can get away from the winter! You could not find a better place in the world for the sport. It's the centre of it all, with Europe just next door. Take the United States. We've just come back from there, and they have just three three-day events in a year, no more. Bruce Davidson had three horses ready to run at Lexington, but was of course only allowed to ride two under the international rules.'

Dual World Champion Davidson's disappointment was Britain's gain, because he and several of his compatriots came on a prolonged tour of British events in the autumn of 1983. The Americans have, says David, another disadvantage too. Lexington, in Kentucky –

*Going . . . going . . . and nearly gone! David Green at the Bull Pens with Mairangi Bay, Badminton 1983 (right to left)*

where the 1978 World Championships were held in such torrid conditions that most of the horses finished in a very distressed condition – is now 'a very boring course. They've made the fences so easy because they are petrified of the same thing happening again. Every person was clear of every fence except one – the water. About fifty per cent had faults there. When you see things like that, it makes you realise how lucky we are to be here.'

David, who was in the Australian team at the 1982 World Championships which finished sixth – together with Andrew Hoy on Davey, the horse with which he won Burghley in 1979, and Mervyn Bennett on Regal Reign – was added to the British long list for Los Angeles when he changed nationality during the winter of 1983. 'The Australian selectors were getting a little bit dirty about me being over here all the time and not doing the selection trials in Australia. Like Jeff McVean' – (the show jumper, who also lives a large part of the time in Britain) – 'who has to go back and ride in a few competitions.' McVean does at least have the advantage of having some horses in Australia as

*Australian Andrew Hoy, winner of Burghley, 1979*

well as in Britain, and also of being sponsored by an Australian who obviously wants him to ride in that country. If David Green had to fly himself and his top horses back to Australia, the cost, in money and time, would be prohibitive.

What are Australia's prospects for Los Angeles? Not too promising, it seems. 'Merv Bennett's got nothing. He's still hoping for Regal Reign, but the horse has not completed an event since the World Championships in Luhmühlen. Wayne Roycroft, who I think is the best in the country by far – you wouldn't want the team to leave the country without him, no matter what he's on – he's not done a one-day or three-day event for a year and a half. Says he's too busy, and reckons just to come out at Melbourne.'

Wayne is a son of the legendary Bill Roycroft, winner of Badminton in 1960 and the man who climbed out of a hospital bed with a broken shoulder during the Rome Olympics to go clear show jumping and ensure his team's gold medal.

Bill is still competing and, at seventy, is just as much of a hero to his compatriots, and others in the game, as he ever was. 'I reckon he's the best horseman in the world. I should think he'll die on a horse: for his sake I hope he does,' says David.

Apparently, whoever they do send, the Australian selectors will not have a woman rider on the team. 'The selectors hate women in teams. They've only ever sent one woman away in a team and said they would never do it again.' Not surprisingly, the husband of the reigning World Champion does not go along with that thinking. But 'iron man' Bill Roycroft once said, after Ireland's Penny Moreton had a fall during the Mexico Games and broke three ribs, 'Even if the horse – which unfortunately was destroyed – had been uninjured and able to go on, nobody would have put Penny back on the horse and sent her on – but they would a man, they would expect him to go on.' It is a valid point of view, and perhaps a typically Australian one.

In the hope that he gets there, David went to the site of the cross-country while he was in Los Angeles in 1983. 'I think the conditions will be all right,' he said. 'But what worries me is the distance. It took us three and a half hours once we were on the freeway out of Los Angeles, and we were not hanging about. How we

are going to walk the course three or four times in the days before I just don't know.'

David and Lucinda keep to their own horses rather than interchanging with each other, though the New-Zealand-bred Mairangi Bay, which Lucinda used to ride, has become David's top international performer. He rode the grey in the 1982 World Championships, when an unfortunate fall put them out of the running, after finishing sixth on him at that year's Badminton, one place higher than Lucinda on Regal Realm, the horse with which she was to take the World title. In July 1982 David and Botany Bay, another ex-Lucinda horse, had a notable triumph at the Irish international event at Punchestown, with his wife second.

They have a fairly clear-cut division of labour in running the yard too, and all that goes with it. While Lucinda, with secretarial help, is attending to the paperwork, entries and so on, David will be outside, mending fences, perhaps building or repairing a practice jump, or doing whatever needs to be done in practical terms to keep the big and expensive operation running smoothly.

But David does not expect to continue this sort of life forever. His father is a fashion photographer and David learned most of the tricks of that trade. 'I worked in the laboratory for some years, colour printing and processing, and then went into the photography side. I did a lot of still life and catalogue work.

'But it's impossible to do that here. I've looked into it, but whenever there's a vacancy there are so many replies, and naturally enough they were going to take a Brit rather than a foreigner. I thought of freelance work, but there's no time in the season.'

But his future does not, as he sees it, lie in photography either. 'We want to end up living back in Australia. Not for might be seven, might be ten years, but I'd much rather bring up a family out there than here. And I can make a living there, which I can't here. I'd go into beef cattle. Land is so much cheaper there – and I hate cities. I like being outdoors.'

But that is a while away yet, and in the meantime the SR Direct Mail's team of Green and Green has a lot to offer eventing fans in both the northern and southern hemispheres.

# 15
# Bute ~ For Better or Worse

In 1978 the drug Phenylbutazone hit the headlines with such force that the shock waves are still being felt today. But why should Phenylbutazone (more commonly known as 'bute') cause such a stir when it is really a miracle drug that kills pain and has benefited many horses?

In the opinion of some riders and owners there is nothing at all wrong with the use of this pain killer; it is its *abuse* that causes journalists to write about it and the authorities to slap fines on riders who have used more than the permitted dosage – and that is hardly the fault of the drug itself.

It would probably have been wrong to have banned its use altogether, as some suggested, and as some countries have done. The FEI has, in fact, got it right in allowing bute to be used to a permitted level (four microgrammes per millilitre of blood plasma). The Bureau of the FEI, and many other people, worked hard to reach a solution and in Berne, on 11 December 1980, they finally put forward a motion – approved by forty-one votes to two – for the use of bute in strictly limited doses.

At the same meeting it was also decided to allow dressage horses to be given bute, a move that no doubt pleased many people because it had previously been banned in that discipline. It was interesting to note, however, that not all the delegates at that important meeting voted for the use of bute; those who dissented when the vote was taken were Sweden and Libya.

It is an undeniable fact that many of the older competition horses in Britain are on bute, and it has been made very clear by some riders that, if they were taken off it, they might not be able to compete. Eventing and show jumping are their life and work, so if bute were to be banned, and these horses suffered pain because of illness or from wear and tear, they would probably be put down.

There are many moral arguments in this particular area. There are those who think both sports should follow racing's lead and ban bute completely. But that would hardly be practical. The antis point out that if a horse has to rely on a pain killer to compete, then he should not be competing, and that if he takes a knock while jumping, he should be allowed time to recover. But that, really, is not the point at issue because any rider who cares about the welfare of his or her horses – and most do – would not allow them to suffer anyway.

Those in favour of the use of bute see nothing wrong in it and some, particularly in show jumping, would like to see the introduction of a 'buffer' zone above the permitted level, raising it from four to eight or ten microgrammes per millilitre of blood plasma. This, they say, would help riders: if tests showed that the level of bute in a horse's blood was within those limits, those involved would receive only a warning and not, perhaps, a fine or ban. However, the authorities are not primarily concerned with the riders: it is the horses who are, rightly, uppermost in their minds.

There is some validity in the riders' arguments, but in reaching the figure of four microgrammes the equestrian officials did take expert veterinary advice, and it must be remembered that the suggested permitted level was put to all national delegates, voted upon and accepted by the majority.

Incidentally, when those who are against bute for competition horses mention racing, they perhaps overlook the fact that not all countries ban its use in that particular sport. It is, in fact, permitted in some states of America and has been for many years.

At this stage it is only right to point out that bute does not make a horse go faster or slower – it simply kills pain. Some racing trainers in Britain might, indeed, use the drug when a horse needs a pain killer and is not actually racing. There is nothing wrong in that as far as the Jockey Club is concerned – so long as the drug does not show up in the animal's blood should he be tested at a racecourse.

Another point to remember is that show jumpers, unlike the majority of racehorses, compete weekly throughout the season, and have to travel great distances when jumping internationally. They are, therefore, more likely to suffer wear and tear, and bute has gone a long way to easing any pain they may suffer.

While making comparisons with racing, one should also bear in mind the fact that hurdlers and steeplechasers do not jump obstacles comprising heavy poles. Hurdlers might snap through the top bar of a flight of hurdles, but chasers just usually brush through the tops of fences. In other words their legs do not have to take the same amount of regular concussion as those of a show jumper.

This is a subject which might well give the authorities in charge of show jumping cause for thought. A move has, indeed, already been made to give jumpers an easier time but it is largely up to individual riders to make sure they do not overwork their mounts.

As a step in the right direction, at the FEI meeting in 1982 it was announced that new regulations had been implemented to reduce the maximum dimensions of obstacles in the Olympic Games. There always has been and always will be concern about the possible over-use and abuse of horses, and to initiate stricter control over the Olympics, where courses are usually very testing, certainly makes good sense. Obviously, if horses are asked too much, in either eventing or show jumping, they stand more chance of injury and, therefore, are more likely to need pain killers.

Nor does it take a genius to realise that lighter poles in show jumping would go a long way to easing the problems faced by the horses. Britain has, indeed, made giant strides in this direction and has, according to at least one top official, introduced not only lighter poles but also shallower cups. Other countries must follow suit, however, if the benefits of such innovations are not to be negated.

To return to the subject of bute itself, when discussing such an emotive subject, it is interesting to study the statistics regarding its use. Those available, at the time of writing, relate to the years 1981 and 1982 and are as follows:

Up to 31 October 1982, a total of 322 horses were tested at forty-four shows and twenty-three jumping horses were found positive to bute – five of those were over the permitted limit. A year earlier, there were 367 tests, of which twenty-six were positive. Three were over the limit.

It could be argued that, as the tests involve about 10 per cent of competing horses, these figures are only a rough guide; nevertheless they are worth studying, and one can draw one's own conclusions.

Unfortunately, it is also a fact that once test samples have been taken, the scientists do seem to take an age to reach a final conclusion, the whole process sometimes taking some sixteen weeks.

There are people who say that if bute was banned altogether for competition horses, as it is in some countries, other drugs might be used, and more horses would undergo neurectomy, an operation to deaden some of the nerves in the hooves or legs. Some show-jumping horses have, in fact, had this operation but many people are very much opposed to it.

There is no doubt that denerving can create both practical and moral problems. It does not attempt to alleviate the original condition, merely to prevent the sensation of pain. Some riders consider that competing on a denerved horse is not totally safe.

Swiss law bans such operations and many people wisely agree. Others, however, point out that even if neurectomy were to be universally outlawed, how would show officials and vets be able to tell, conclusively, that a horse had been denerved? The arguments continue, both for and against, and look like doing so for a considerable time.

At least with bute there is a form of control, because when tests are taken – as they frequently are at international shows – veterinary officials are usually able to tell exactly how much of the drug has been administered and whether it is below or above the permitted level.

There is, of course, always the danger that such a controversial subject will be over-dramatised by those who have only a cursory knowledge of the subject. When that happens people involved in eventing and show jumping are entitled to ask what right outsiders have to make suggestions that may concern their and their horses' future and welfare.

On the other hand, those who have done their home-work might reasonably argue that some people are altogether too close to the subject, and their opinions are bound to be tinged with bias because they have personal interests at stake.

It must, ultimately, be left to the authorities, that is, the FEI, an organisation which is concerned about all matters in equestrianism, making what it considers to be the correct decisions, and putting the horse first.

Putting horses first, whatever anyone thinks, is the right moral attitude to adopt because we all have a duty to look after the animals we use for sport. They must be treated with care, and are most certainly not there to be abused, either for money, or for any other reason.

*Prince Philip, President of the FEI, at Lexington in 1978*

Under the leadership of Prince Philip, who has agreed to continue as President despite planning to retire this year after twenty years, the FEI, with its finger on the pulse of all major issues, has done a remarkable, responsible job.

Each national equestrian federation comes under the protective umbrella of the FEI and it all works well. If, however, each country wished to go its own way, the system could not possibly work and major issues, such as the ones discussed in this chapter, would be far harder to resolve.

The FEI has shown the way ahead and the good work will continue, even though, with subjects such as bute and denerving operations, there will always be a difference of opinion.

Matters came to a head for riders with horses on bute in 1978 when it was suggested at the FEI General Assembly in Paris that Phenylbutazone, and other non-steroid anti-inflammatory drugs, be added to the list of Prohibited Substances published by the FEI from 1 January 1981. But those drawing up the agenda did make it absolutely clear that veterinary evidence, not then available, should be placed before the Bureau.

The questions they wanted answered were: whether the use of such drugs, or any particular one, does or does not affect the performance of a horse; whether or not harmful side-effects were produced in the animal; and whether the quantity of such drugs when administered could be estimated with accuracy to enable their use to be controlled as to quantity and effect.

It was then made absolutely clear that the matter could again be brought before the assembly to determine whether the date (January 1981) should be postponed, or whether other regulations could be drafted.

I have quoted from the proposals at the assembly in Paris because it was highly relevant at the time, and worried many riders in Britain and, in particular, two major officials, too; they were Major General Jack Reynolds, CB, OBE, director general of the British Equestrian Federation, and Colonel Sir Harry Llewellyn.

*Major General Jack Reynolds, whose hard efforts helped with the bute question*

At one stage Sir Harry burst into print, telling people that if bute was to be banned then for many horses it would mean the bullet. Strong words, but from the heart and most certainly meant. It was after the meeting in Paris that Major General Reynolds and Sir Harry put the wheels into motion that were to help change the whole course of thinking by the majority of delegates affiliated to the FEI.

Prince Philip was approached, and agreed that the essential veterinary evidence (if indeed it was there)

*Lieutenant Colonel Sir Harry Llewellyn, a firm advocate of bute*

should be presented. It was also pointed out that, whatever action was taken, the FEI was not prepared to fund it.

'Then,' said Major General Reynolds, 'in conjunction with Jim Cunningham, who was President of the BEVA (British Equine Veterinary Association), a programme was arranged with the Royal Veterinary College to look into the practicability of quantitative testing of bute and the establishment of possible acceptable levels.

'This work was funded by the British Equestrian Federation and two pharmaceutical companies, and cost just in excess of £10,000.

'The results of this study, and work carried out by the Americans (on the racing side) and some Germans and Swiss, was examined by a special FEI panel. After many internal discussions, papers were prepared for the General Assembly of December that year (1980).

'Prior to this, Prince Philip addressed the BEVA Congress on 4 December, giving the administrators' point of view.'

Instead of banning the drug outright, everyone concerned appeared to see the value of the research. But if it had not been for the Major General, Sir Harry and their colleagues, one can only assume that bute might well have been banned from competition horses. There had been an outcry about the use of drugs generally in sport and the FEI had made the correct move at the right time.

But when it looked as if bute might be banned there were many worried people in the horse world. And even though it can now legally be used, within the stipulated limits, some riders maintain it is difficult to check whether or not more than four microgrammes have, in fact, been given to a horse.

Having spoken to many of those who do use bute, I find the concensus of opinion seems to be that, for the majority of jumpers, just under one sachet is sufficient to keep within the rules. But horses do differ: some can take more than others, and an amount which registers over the limit for one tested horse might not do so in the case of another. That is one of the reasons why David Broome, on behalf of the International Riders Club in show jumping, was among those who wanted a 'buffer' zone introduced.

In 1982 several riders were fined because their horses failed dope tests by exceeding the prescribed level. In some of the cases, it was noted, the level was only just over. It was, however, sufficient to break the rules, so fines were levied and, in one case at least, a ban imposed. There is no doubt that there are competitors who think they are hard done by, particularly when they have done their best to make sure their horse, or horses, have not been given too much bute.

The only answer, as the rules stand, is to make sure that the correct dosage is given. Riders should work out, with veterinary help, the right amount for their own horses – even if it means having special measuring spoons made so that they hold exactly the permitted dosage. Then, at least, mistakes would be less frequent.

It is difficult and can lead to a lot of bad feeling when a rider is fined because a dope test has proved positive – particularly if everyone knows that the person concerned is honest and would not knowingly cheat.

But the trouble with a buffer zone is, where do you draw the line? If, after extensive veterinary tests, four microgrammes per millilitre of blood plasma is considered right, what is the point of making a rule and then changing the amount?

If, however, after spending more than £10,000 on research, the veterinary scientists had failed to establish any sound conclusions, it might have been a different matter and the drug might have been banned for good, in all competition horses. What would riders who use bute have done then?

Those who fought hard to retain it say that it is far better to have strict control, than not to have bute at all and, when anyone has gone into the subject deeply, it is reasoning which is very difficult to deny.

There are riders who will keep on trying to get things changed, and that is their prerogative. But it is unlikely that the FEI will alter its rules after going into the subject of bute so thoroughly.

As Major General Jack Reynolds says, 'It is an emotive issue, and it was judged better to remain at four microgrammes per millilitre than face a chance of the drug being banned altogether.'

# 16
# Man with the Golden Touch

Ask anyone interested in equestrian sport which British rider has won more Olympic gold medals than any other and they are sure to come up with the right answer: Richard Meade. The winner of three golds – two team and one individual – he is much respected and admired in every country where eventing is popular, and has earned a place among the greats, both for his remarkable talent of being able to ride any horse well, and for his winning prowess.

Those who saw him ride in the 1972 Munich Olympic Games, where he won two of his three gold medals, will never forget his epic round across country. Meade rode Major Derek Allhusen's home-bred Laurieston and became the first person in British equestrian history to win an individual gold medal. It was an incredibly moving moment for the British fans, and a great personal achievement for Richard. In the dressage phase he had 50.67 penalty points which put him in seventh place, and when he set off across country he was told to go fast and clear. Considering what had befallen several riders beforehand, this seemed a tall order – even for a man of Meade's experience and standing.

For these Olympic Games the West Germans had installed an indicator board with coloured tabs at the top that flashed up when a rider had a fall, or a refusal, or cleared a fence. It was a brilliant piece of machinery because it allowed fans to follow the progress of all the riders from one vantage point.

Meade started out on the cross-country, the first flash indicator came up green, and British fans held their breath as, one by one, the others followed suit. As the last green came up on the board everyone knew that, unless a miracle happened for someone else, the British team would be in the lead and Meade would be well on his way to an individual gold.

Italy's Alessandro Argenton on Woodland went well, too, finishing the day in second place behind Meade, with Sweden's Jan Jonsson in third on Sarajevo and Mary Gordon-Watson with Cornishman V fourth. The Germans had built a very good course and, of the seventy-three who started, only twenty-three failed to finish the cross-country. In contrast with some other major events in recent years, not one horse was killed or badly injured.

In the show-jumping phase, that stood between Britain and final victory, forty-eight starters took on the twelve fences built by Micky Brinkmann, and Meade had just one fence in hand. But, even though the British fans were gripping their seats, hoping, some perhaps praying that all would go well, they had no real need to worry: Meade, and his intelligent, brave horse, sailed over every fence without error and, to rapturous applause, galloped into the history books.

For any youngster dreaming of Olympic fame the Munich Games are the ones to be studied in depth because they encompassed everything of sporting value. Unfortunately, however, they will not be remembered chiefly for the athletic glory because it was during these Games that the Black September terrorists slaughtered several Israeli athletes, an event which stunned the world. Many thought that the Games should have been called off, but in fact they were allowed to continue.

Richard Meade's first gold medal had come in 1968, when he rode Cornishman V at the Mexico Olympics. On that occasion the team had to contend with a storm that almost wrecked the event – one horse was, in fact, drowned. It was also a bad time politically: before the Games started hundreds of demonstrating students had been machine-gunned. It was an incident which destroyed the spirit of the Games, but like Munich four years on, they were allowed to continue.

But Mexico, with all its political unrest and bad weather, was not the first Olympics for Meade; he had been chosen to represent Britain four years earlier in Tokyo on a horse called Barberry, who so very nearly gave him success at the first time of asking. For, after the dressage and cross-country phases, Meade held the lead by just one point. But in the final show-jumping section Barberry, probably feeling the effects of the speed and endurance test, started to make mistakes, and when he knocked two fences down and then had a refusal, Meade dropped rapidly down the line to eighth place. It was, nevertheless, a fine effort.

That brilliant ride across country had been enough to make those who knew anything about eventing sit up and take notice; here was a young man destined to reach the very top because of his intelligence and brilliance in the saddle. Even then the magic ingredient which all champions must have was there for all to see: the ability to keep calm under severe pressure. Some people, faced with overwhelming responsibility, go to pieces. The mind goes blank, the pressure eats away at them like a cancer until it is too much to bear and they crack. It is not a condemnation of them, because most people would feel the same under similar circumstances – only those who are rather special can cope. In equestrianism some riders can face up to the ultimate test: Meade is such a man.

In Munich he knew that for Britain to have any chance of winning gold medals, he was the one who had to deliver; the words 'go fast and clear' must have been ringing in his ears as he set out on the cross-country, but not once did he falter. This is a quality which cannot be taught. Meade has it in abundance – and a lot more besides. That is why, to this day, it can almost be guaranteed that in any British team for which Meade is chosen to ride, he will be going at number four. The *chef d'équipe* must be absolutely certain that whoever goes last can be relied on, without question,

*Richard Meade and Laurieston on their way to winning the Olympic individual and team golds at Munich in 1972*

knowing his performance can mean the difference between winning and losing.

During 1969 Meade took over the ride on The Poacher, winning Badminton on him for the first time in 1970. The pair went on to greater honours that same year by helping the British team to win the World Championship in Punchestown; then, in 1971, they were in the winning European Championship team at Burghley. The Poacher, who had given so much service to his country, was subsequently retired.

*Time to relax with the family – Richard and Angela Meade, at home with baby James*

Although Meade has won Badminton twice, it could well have been three times had things gone according to plan in 1972, before his gold-medal-winning ride at Munich. He was ahead on the final day, but when Mark Phillips went clear in the show-jumping phase on Great Ovation, it meant that Meade had absolutely no room for error and had to go clear to win. He did, in fact, get round without error but in doing so went wide on the bends and finished outside the time allowed and was given time penalties. The majority of the spectators were stunned when the commentator gave the result over the loudspeaker system: Phillips had finished with a total of 106.60 penalty points, while Meade had 107.25. It was dreadful for Meade and his mount Laurieston, and few people would have taken the defeat with good grace. But, after Phillips had won this, his second Badminton in succession, Meade was the first person to congratulate him.

After that defeat Meade said of his mistake, 'You make an error like that once in your life and never again.' It would have taken some riders an age to recover from a blow like that, but not Meade who, at the Olympics later in the year, was winning gold medals. The following year he went to Boekelo, in Holland, and won the major international there on Wayfarer II, this time reversing the form with Phillips who finished second.

Meade's 1973 Badminton ride was to have been Wayfarer, but the horse developed leg trouble and it looked as though the triple Olympic gold medallist would be without a mount. But then his luck changed and Barbara Hammond, who was side-lined, offered him the ride on her Eagle Rock. After a very good partnership across country Meade was in third place behind Lucinda Prior-Palmer on Be Fair and Marjorie Comerford on The Ghillie. The course had taken its toll, and a total of twenty-three had failed to finish. Meade moved up a place after the show-jumping phase, Marjorie Comerford suffering appalling luck and dropped right down the placings when The Ghillie had three fences down. The eventual victor was Lucinda, who was winning Badminton for the first time.

Later that year Wayfarer came sound again and was picked to represent Britain in the European Championships in Kiev. Meade's ability to remain calm under pressure certainly paid off here and while dozens of riders fell at the notorious fence two, Meade and Wayfarer attacked it heartily, sailing over as though they had wings and eventually finishing fourth overall.

However, many people remember Meade not for the first-class ride he gave Wayfarer, but for the fact that, having fathomed out the problems of fence two and the way to approach it, early in the competition, he then spent a great deal of time running backwards and forwards helping his team-mates by telling them what the majority of other riders were doing and the mistakes

*Kiev held no fear for Richard as he safely negotiated the dreaded fence two at the European Championships, on Wayfarer*

they were making. That underlined Meade's deep concern for his colleagues and the fact that he always has the team effort at heart. What happened in Kiev is now history, but the display of courage shown by all will never be forgotten and our team's bronze medal was certainly won with talent and bravery.

If a rider is intent on being a winner he or she must be in top physical condition, for to hold a horse together during the speed and endurance test is no easy task. A rider who is not one hundred per cent fit cannot do his horse justice. One thing in Richard Meade's favour is

the fact that he keeps himself supremely fit. Even when he lived in London he could be seen in the early hours of the morning pounding the pavements or running hard around the parks. In May 1977 he was married to Angela Farquhar and now lives in the country at Church Farm, West Littleton, Wiltshire.

Many people consider that the only way to get fit to ride is to ride horses as often as possible, and while there is a lot of truth in this, the fact is that running does help to strengthen the muscles and keep the lungs clear. Many National Hunt jockeys, who regularly ride winners, still don a tracksuit and run several miles a day. The same thing could benefit any rider competing in eventing.

One of the biggest tests for any rider is to live up to

Above: *Meade the man of action, here on Three Cups at Badminton, 1982*

Opposite: *Meade and Andeguy winners at Boekelo, Holland, 1983*

the opinions others have of him and, in this respect, too, Richard Meade comes through with flying colours.

'First and foremost,' said someone who has known him for years, 'he is a perfect gentleman, and always has been. He also cares deeply about others and would always put them before himself. He is also never too busy to help the younger generation with advice and that is just one of the reasons he is so well liked in the sport.' They are accolades that Meade would certainly shy away from, but they happen to be true and the man is certainly a credit to a sport he loves.

Instead of levelling off, as so many pastimes do, eventing continues to go from strength to strength because of the high calibre of people involved with it. Perhaps one of the reasons for this is the fact that the majority of people in the sport are true amateurs and have not been spoiled by great amounts of prize money. Sponsors are, of course, of vital importance and the fact that the first prize money at both Badminton and

*Taking it all in his stride, Richard Meade and Kilcashel in full flight*

Burghley is £5000 is much appreciated by all concerned. But prizes of that sort are not generally available and so riders are not forever chasing big cash awards. They ride horses across country because that is what they want to do – not because of financial incentives. It is all vastly different from show jumping, where there is more than a million pounds available in prize money each year, with the best riders competing for it week in and week out throughout the season.

But few riders, no matter how good, can afford to compete at top level in eventing now, without the support of sponsorship. It can cost anything up to £6000 to keep one horse in training and that can be a crushing financial burden.

In Meade's case it was George Wimpey Ltd who stepped in to sponsor him in 1980; the company has had a tremendous run of success with him. It does, however, work both ways because although the rider is helped

*Deep in the saddle and going strong, Richard Meade and Speculator over the Whitbread Drays at Badminton, 1982*

out with the massive expenses eventing always involves, the sponsor gets his just reward by frequent mentions in the newspapers and on television. With a man like Meade, those mentions happen with regularity and, therefore, George Wimpey Ltd receives frequent mentions in the media along with him.

Unlike in show jumping, it is surprising that those who put up the money do not demand that the top riders be allowed to attach prefixes to their horses' names. It is, perhaps, just a matter of time before eventing catches up in this respect.

As any event rider will confirm, everything is most certainly not glamour in their sport. All too often along with the good times come the inevitable bad ones and mishaps which must be taken in one's stride. Little did Richard Meade know, for instance, in the autumn of 1982 he would suffer an extraordinary accident at Burghley. During the roads and tracks phase it is common practice for a rider to give his mount a rest and save his energy for the cross-country phase by running alongside the horse for part of the way. It is a wise policy and a typical example of how fit an event rider has to be.

At the 1982 Burghley meeting Meade had dismounted from Three Cups and was jogging along beside him when suddenly the horse stumbled and stood on his rider's right foot; a metal stud in the horse's shoe was driven into the base of Meade's toes, and the pain must have been excruciating; but, with great fortitude, he continued, and then rode the twenty-seven-fence cross-country course in what must have been sheer agony. He did not win, but to have continued in the way he did was considered by many to be both brave and brilliant.

It was in that year that Meade and Kilcashel made the trip to Luhmühlen and helped the British team to win the World Championship, Lucinda Green making it a memorable occasion by winning the individual title on Regal Realm.

A year later, however, Meade was to retire his gallant old warrior Speculator, a winner at Badminton and a horse who had tackled that formidable event five times. When Meade first started riding Speculator he knew that if he could get the horse fully under control, he could be a very good jumper indeed and, after a few traumatic experiences, he was proved right when the gelding won Badminton in 1982. Winning the Whitbread Trophy is never easy but to have won it with 'Spec', as Meade fondly called him, was a great pleasure to him. But his retirement meant that Meade was without a mount for Badminton in 1983.

His riding career has encompassed many prizes, including the Horseman of the Year Award, presented by the National Sporting Club in 1973, and the British Equestrian Writers Association has also honoured him. He was awarded the OBE in 1974.

The traditional British system has regularly thrown up great riders like Richard Meade but that is all being threatened nowadays by the proposed ban on foxhunting. Riding to hounds has always been the ideal way of teaching young horses – and riders – how to cope with the unexpected across country, and if hunting were to be banned it could damage the sport of eventing irrevocably.

As far as the anti brigade is concerned that probably does not matter, but if Britain does not encourage young talent, then we are bound to slip into the sport's second division. And if we cannot produce more riders like Richard Meade, then we can forget all about winning gold medals.

# 17
# The Horse Trials Group and the British Horse Society

There are more than 4000 horses registered with the British Horse Society Horse Trials Group at the British Equestrian Centre, Stoneleigh, in Warwickshire, and it is from this wealth of talent that our champions of the future will come.

At the moment many are only novices and still have a long way to go before reaching the heights of top-class eventing; they still have to negotiate intermediate and advanced one-day and two-day trials before attempting the biggest test of all, the international three-day event.

But this system, controlled and directed by the Horse Trials Group Committee, is one of the main reasons why Britain produces some of the very best horses and riders in the world, and yet keeps the grass roots of the sport on a healthy, progressive level.

Anyone who wants to event seriously in this country must be a full member of the British Horse Society and of the Horse Trials Group, and their horses must be registered with the latter. All members receive regular news bulletins, schedules and fixture cards and, more importantly perhaps, have the right to elect half of the Horse Trials Committee, a sensible and democratic arrangement.

Members may also attend the annual November Group conference, at which they can express their own opinions; it is a highly-informative and sometimes very entertaining meeting.

The director of Horse Trials is Tim Taylor, who took over in 1984, and the Chairman of the Horse Trials Group Committee is Martin Whiteley, a man much to be admired for all the excellent work he does on behalf of the sport. And those on the committee with him are all men who care deeply about eventing. At the time of writing they are: Colonel Hubert Allfrey, MC, TD, DL; Chris Collins; The Earl of Cottenham; Richard Meade, OBE; Major Lawrence Rook; Lord

*Life has its moments – Martin Whiteley at Frauenfeld in 1983*

Above: *Then a top rider, Martin Whiteley in action on The Poacher at Burghley in 1965. Ben Jones won a team gold medal at the 1968 Mexico Olympics on the same horse*

Opposite: *Hold on there! The Earl of Cottenham, a member of the Horse Trials committee, on Kinallen at Badminton in 1973*

Hugh Russell; Christopher Schofield, OBE; Michael Tucker; John Tulloch and Lieutenant Colonel Frank Weldon, MVO, MBE, MC. An impressive group of people, they are experts in eventing, believe passionately in what they are doing, and have all played a part in making Britain one of the strongest nations at the sport.

Martin Whiteley, a former top rider, became chairman of the committee in 1980. After schooldays at Eton (where he is a housemaster), he joined the Army and eventually found himself serving in Germany. It was there that he rode on the flat and over jumps. Then a horse called St Nicholas changed his life and he became interested in eventing. But it was The Poacher who helped him win a team gold medal and the individual silver in the 1967 European Championships. The Poacher was a great horse, who played a significant part in keeping Britain at the top of eventing. In the 1968 Olympics, held in Mexico, Whiteley could have ridden The Poacher himself; but, typically, he stood down when Sergeant Ben Jones' horse Foxdor suddenly died, and put his mount at the disposal of the selectors. Jones went on to win a team gold medal.

Another man whose experience is so valuable to the sport is Chris Collins, who heads the Selection Committee. He rode eventing and is a former champion amateur National Hunt jockey, the winner of many races both in Britain and abroad.

*Chris Collins with Henrietta Knight and Ann Starkey (partly obscured)*

The job of the Selection Committee is, perhaps, one of the most difficult because with its members lies much of the responsibility for the success or failure of the British teams. The selectors must know each rider and horse; they must be able to assess who will do well in a championship as an individual, who would be best passed over as a team member. They must decide what is best for the team as a whole – personalities must not enter into it. Every squad of riders must be picked on merit and nothing else. It is the horse and rider combination that counts all the way down the line: no matter how brilliant the rider, he cannot get very far

without a suitable horse, and if one is not readily available then his chances of success are nil.

It is hardly surprising when one considers how brilliantly many of the men on the Horse Trials Group Committee rode, and, in some cases, still do ride, both at home and abroad, that they know just what is required to keep Britain at the top.

Those in command have their fingers firmly on the pulse of all matters relating to eventing. They have travelled many thousands of miles and visited many different countries on behalf of our international riders. For, as with a major battle, in order to win, the whole campaign must be thought out and planned from beginning to end before the action actually starts. Only in this way can everyone know what they are doing and exactly what is expected of them, right down to the final detail. That the Horse Trials Group has been right is amply demonstrated by the number of medals our teams have won over the years.

One of the Group's most valuable assets is its great organising ability. As can be seen at any international event, even one mistake, silly or otherwise, can literally mean the difference between victory and defeat. It is remarkable how many other nations do not bother to organise themselves properly, or seem to take unnecessary risks. Such a cavalier attitude can sometimes work, but, more often than not, victory and all that goes with it is due to forward planning and a lot of hard work on the part of all connected with the team.

And this is where the loyal fans of eventing must be given a special mention, because many of these stalwarts travel all over the world, at great personal expense, to give our riders much-needed and well-deserved support. It is highly encouraging for competitors to hear and see that support, particularly when the going gets tough, and no praise is too high for these people – they are the very life-blood of the sport without whom eventing could not continue to thrive.

As has already been mentioned, the sport of horse trials comes under the umbrella of the British Horse Society, which is a registered charity set up to look after the interests of both riders and horses throughout the United Kingdom. It is an organisation that is the envy of many other societies throughout the world.

The president and former chairman of the British Horse Society is Dorian Williams, OBE, a man of great courage and remarkable skills, who is totally dedicated to his work. Apart from his magnificent efforts on behalf of the BHS, he is also an author, broadcaster, playwright, actor and master of foxhounds. He is a man who cares deeply about others and devotes much of his free time to helping various charities. It was fitting that he should follow in the footsteps of his father, Colonel V. D. S. Williams, OBE, who was himself president of the British Horse Society in 1953.

As a commentator on eventing and show jumping Dorian helped bring both sports into the homes of millions, with a voice that will never be forgotten by equestrian fans. Even when he was very ill, during the early seventies, he still made the trip to the Ukraine to commentate on the European three-day event Championships. It took a great deal of courage and fortitude on his part and he is a man who commands much respect from all who know him.

There have been many great people who have taken on the task of being president of the British Horse Society including, in recent years, Her Grace Lavinia, Duchess of Norfolk, CBE; Mr E. Holland-Martin; The Right Honourable The Earl of March and Kinrara; The Earl of Westmorland, KCVO; General Sir John Mogg, GCB, CBE, DSO; and the Marquess of Abergavenny, KG, OBE, JP, MFH.

And so the list goes on, right back to 1948, when Mr W. J. Cumber, CBE, was the very first president of the Society. It was only eight years later that HRH The Prince Philip, Duke of Edinburgh, KG, took his turn for a year in office. Current chairman of the BHS is Peter Fenwick, a man much admired by those who work for him at the British Equestrian Centre.

Apart from promoting equestrian sport and helping to organise, under the various committees, the running of them, the British Horse Society also takes on the role of welfare officer. And that is no easy task with the number of horses there are in Great Britain. However, every complaint is looked into by those concerned and if something has to be put right, then that is exactly what happens. It is true to say that the BHS is labour intensified, but then it has to be in order to cope properly with the multitude of questions that are asked of it.

Without the BHS or the Horse Trials Group Committee, eventing as we know it today could not exist. For any sport to prosper and thrive, it must produce winners and that is why Britain is one of the strongest eventing nations in the world. But that success has not simply been due to the efforts of our riders and horses. Without an overall plan, and major long-term policies, the whole structure could not possibly survive. That is, indeed, where those at Stoneleigh come in, and although most of their work is done behind the scenes, with very little publicity, it is vital to the very existence of all horse sports, and eventing in particular.

For any association to be able to exist, it must have the backing of the public, something the BHS attracts

*Dorian Williams, President of the British Horse Society*

because it offers value for money and many important benefits. For example, all members have automatic third-party insurance; special rates for horse, car and horsebox insurance are also available and there is a discount buying scheme. Other benefits include the use of the members' tent at the Badminton Horse Trials and a special members' tea-tent at Burghley. To some these privileges may seem small but, in fact, they make a great difference to those who visit the two major trials mentioned.

On top of all that, members have the right to attend and vote at the Annual General Meeting. At the latter members are able to air their points of view and maybe, if they are strong enough and they are in the right, they will be able to bring about changes. That is one of the very good things about the BHS – those in charge are always prepared to listen to someone else's point of view.

*Germany's Karl Schultz and Madrigal, showing how a dressage test should be ridden*

The more people who belong to the BHS, the stronger it becomes and the more good it is able to do for horses. There are various scales of membership, but all subscriptions are inclusive of VAT and the joining fee is, at the time of writing, £5.75. On top of that, full annual adult membership for those aged twenty-one or over is an additional £11.00. But for junior membership (under twenty-one) it is just £7.00. Life membership is also available and is easy to arrange; the cost is from £400 down to £50, depending on the applicant's age. These prices are, of course, subject to change.

To join, all you have to do is write to the Secretary, British Horse Society, The British Equestrian Centre, Stoneleigh, Kenilworth, Warwickshire. It is as simple as that and the benefits are there for all to see.

Another of the disciplines which comes under the BHS umbrella, is dressage, whose committee chairman is Diana Mason. For years Britain lagged behind the Germans in this sport, but now, slowly but surely our riders are beginning to make their presence felt at international level. As dressage is one of the three phases of eventing, it has always been of interest to horse trials riders. Particularly successful is Rachel Bayliss, winner of the individual gold medal in the 1983 European Horse Trials Championships at Frauenfeld. So good is her dressage that at Badminton in 1983 she scored a 30 in the test with Mystic Minstrel. The test was so good that Anton Bühler, the Swiss president of the jury, included a maximum score of 10. Miss Bayliss did not win the event, but if she had had luck on her side she could have proved to all, as indeed she did in the European Championships, how important dressage is in eventing.

It is interesting to note that Nils Haagensen, who won the individual European title in Luhmühlen, was a member of the Danish dressage team at the 1976 Olympic Games. That proves beyond doubt that if a rider is brilliant at dressage, and can master both the cross-country phases and the show-jumping section, he has a better chance than most of winning titles.

Another outstanding three-day-event dressage rider is Karl Schultz who, on the incredible Madrigal, invariably held a big lead after the first phase of international events. At Burghley, in the European Championships of 1977, it helped them to win a silver medal.

*Rachel Bayliss and Mystic Minstrel now rival the Germans at dressage, and often beat them*

The Germans, like the British, have their own national equestrian plans, but many people believe the British Horse Society, by keeping all the equestrian sports under its protective wing, has found the true secret of success.

# 18
# Vital Support

Money is always a problem in amateur sport, not so much the winning of it, but having enough to keep going without making too many sacrifices. In eventing, like show jumping, the expenses can be crippling and any financial help is always welcomed, particularly in this day and age. But who do the youngsters in horse

*Jane Pontifex – a hard worker for the Horse Trials Support Group and writer for* Horse and Hound

trials go to for backing when they perhaps have only one horse and a name the general public does not recognise? They can hardly approach major companies and expect to be given thousands of pounds. They must, quite rightly, be able to convince those concerned that the money they are being asked to give away will be wisely spent, and will benefit the company.

Those youngsters who do try to gain sponsorship through their own efforts are to be congratulated, but the chances of obtaining any are remote. That is why the Horse Trials Support Group is so important because it is made up of people who want to play a personal, active part in helping to promote young riders to the ranks of Britain's international three-day-event team. It is an altruistic organisation, with high ideals, and its members typify the sort of person who believes totally in British eventing and the young people in it. We are fortunate that there are still such people willing to help.

The honorary secretary is Miss Jane Pontifex, who writes about eventing in *Horse and Hound*. Jane is very close to the horse trials riders and her work on their behalf is much appreciated. She says, 'The annual subscription rate for individual members is £100, or £150 for husband and wife, in the Horse Trials Support Group, and we are very lucky because membership is increasing all the time.'

That is good news because they are all doing a fine job, and go out of their way to make people welcome, particularly at Badminton where they have their own hospitality marquee, run by Mrs Rosemary Barlow, who has helped to make it a great success. 'Frank

Weldon gives us the site,' says Jane, 'and we pay for the tent. Radio Rentals also help out and give us the use of closed-circuit television, which is very kind of them.

'We decided to have a hospitality tent, because we feel that personal contact helps to bring in new members and publicity helps, too, because reading something about the Group can sometimes fire people's enthusiasm.'

The Horse Trials Support Group came into being in 1978 and has flourished ever since. It is just what was needed and, like all good ideas, it has been created to last. Because it has been built on firm foundations, and is run by people who know what they are doing, it will do just that.

The chairman is Major Lawrence Rook, a tall, dignified man who was a former top-class-event rider, and a person who is deeply involved in the horse trials world. The other members of the Horse Trials Support Group, in an official capacity, are The Earl of Cottenham, Bob Dean, Lieutenant Colonel Tom Greenhalgh, Tim Holderness-Roddam, Chris Collins (as chairman of the Selection Committee) and Martin Whiteley (ex officio, as chairman of the Horse Trials Committee). All good men and true, who are held in high regard by those both in and out of the sport.

But how does the Horse Trials Group work, and how do they go about choosing who should receive their help? The Selection Committee submits to the Horse Trials Support Group the names of riders recommended for a grant. Once a grant has been allocated the rider, or riders, are expected to be guided by a member of the Selection Committee, who is specifically appointed to discuss, and advise on, their individual training plans and competition programme, and also to monitor their expenditure. It is a good way of doing things, and is most helpful to all concerned.

The whole point is, the Group cares enough to offer positive, financial help and, at the same time, give members of the public the opportunity to contribute if they want to. Many people in this country love eventing and want to help, but do not know how to go about it. That is just one of the reasons that make the Horse Trials Support Group so necessary for riders and fans alike.

Virginia Holgate, one of our most talented event riders, is an excellent example of how the policy of encouraging young riders works. Miss Holgate, a former Junior European Champion, showed tremendous ability with two of her horses, and was helped by the Support Group during the 1980–81 season. She became a valuable member of the British team which won the European Championship in 1981, and then, because she was

so talented, secured commercial sponsorship of four horses for the following three years. Miss Holgate was also a member of the squad which won the World Championship in West Germany in 1982, and is, without question, a great asset to British eventing. She also won Burghley in 1983. It was right that the Horse Trials Support Group helped her during those early years. Along with their advisers they spotted her talent, and backed their judgement, which proved correct.

The Selection Committee, appointed in 1980, under the chairmanship of Chris Collins, no longer follows a policy of acquiring horses but aims to direct support to riders themselves, which is what they did with Virginia Holgate. The first chairman of the Support Group was Martin Whiteley, a position he held until he became chairman of the Horse Trials Committee in 1981.

*Major Lawrence Rook, heads the Horse Trials Support Group*

*Virginia Holgate was helped by the Horse Trials Support Group during the 1980–81 season and has gone on to great things; seen here on Priceless at the World Championships in Luhmühlen, 1982, where she was a member of the victorious British gold-medal-winning team*

But what do the members of the public actually get for their money, apart from a great deal of personal satisfaction from knowing they are giving an enormous amount of much-needed help to others? The answer is many valuable assets, including membership of the British Horse Society's Horse Trials Group, based at Stoneleigh in Warwickshire, which sends out fixture lists, and official information on the general developments in the sport. This is all important if you want to keep your finger on the pulse of progress.

Then there is membership of the Burghley Horse Trials in Stamford, Lincolnshire, and a season's pass for a central car park at the Badminton Horse Trials with use, of course, of the tent, bar and closed-circuit television.

On top of that there is the annual dinner, for which members pay, and to which they may invite guests; an

*Fiona Moore is one of those to have benefited from the efforts of the Horse Trials Support Group; seen here on Kilgowan Lad safely negotiating the rails at Burghley, 1983*

annual general meeting, probably at Burghley, where all members, if they so wish, may raise subjects for discussion. Then there is the periodic newsletter on the Support Group's overall plans and activities, and a report from the chairman of the Selection Committee. This way everyone is involved in what is happening, and this is why it is so successful.

Other activities, both social and fund raising, may be planned from time to time and facilities provided (such as a tour to the annual CCIO). In short, the organisers want their members to feel as though they belong to a club, so that they can experience and be involved in the sport of eventing, and watch the progress of the riders they have helped. It is all great fun, particularly when members turn up at Badminton and have lunch and drinks in their own hospitality tent. Everyone, including guests, is made welcome. If they wish, they can, while having coffee, tea or perhaps something stronger, watch cross-country day in comfort, should they not feel like walking from fence to fence. It is entirely up to the individual, but the splendid amenities are always there for those who wish to take advantage of them.

The object of the exercise is to encourage more people to become members, and the only way to do that properly, and in the numbers that make it all justifiable, is to provide good value. The sport itself plays its part by producing riders who win, not only at home, but on the international scene as well. Winning, or doing well, creates publicity, which in turn promotes the sport and makes people sit up and take notice of what is going on.

There is, however, a big gap between those who prove themselves in the junior ranks as riders, and others who have already made names for themselves in the big league.

It is relevant here to quote from the Support Group's pamphlet: 'In the three-day-event world, the competition is becoming keener and the standard is rising all the time and so are the costs involved in attaining that standard.

'Britain has an outstanding record of international success, yet, while most countries give government grants to their teams, selection for the British team is now almost out of reach of even the most talented riders unless they have strong financial backing. Luckily, eventing enjoys such popularity at present that most of our top riders – those who have already made a name for themselves at Badminton or Burghley, or in three-day events abroad – are able to attract commercial sponsorship of their own.

'But those in the next rank – the younger riders who have proved their worth in junior or national compe-

titions, but have not yet caught the public eye – can do little more to help themselves. They need funds, not only for the upkeep of two or three horses at least, but also for the further training and opportunity for advanced competition that could carry them to the top.

'It is these riders, picked out by the Horse Trials Selection Committee, whom the Support Group has agreed to make its special responsibility: riders who have gone about as far as they can on their own but who, with concerted help, are capable of becoming the team members of the future.'

That, in fact, is one of the best ways to help out young, promising event riders – there is nothing worse than knowing what you want to do, having the ability to do it, then being thwarted by not having the money available to carry on in top-flight competition.

The government does make a contribution to sport, through the Sports Council, and horse trials do benefit – the money being used to help send our equestrian teams abroad to compete.

We also have, in this country, the British International Equestrian Fund, and the Support Group plays an independent role within the framework of the BIEF. It all works extremely well and to the riders' benefit.

The British International Equestrian Fund does a brilliant fund-raising job and without its hard-working organisers, Britain's equestrians could not hope to operate on the scale they do now. It costs hundreds of thousands of pounds to send our Olympic hopefuls abroad, to give them valuable experience, before the Games actually take place. The Sports Council cash helps, but it is largely the money pulled in through fund raising that makes it all possible. That is why it is so important for the public to become involved and enjoy their eventing because without them, to compete internationally would be a lot harder than it is at present.

However, it is not just a question of going to people and flatly asking them for money. It is a lot more sophisticated than that, and to keep the cash flowing the organisers have to keep coming up with a series of good ideas that will encourage donations, no matter how small. Unlike in ancient Greece, the Olympics now cost millions to stage and, like everything else, the price of gold medals is always going up, particularly for the eventers. To win at the Olympics, as Britain knows from past experience, takes special horses and riders.

Before going to any Olympic Games, horses and riders must have first earned selection on the home front at trials like Badminton, and proved their worth abroad on the international scene. It is the only way, and travelling to other countries takes a great deal of money. That is why, years before any Olympics, the fund raisers and in particular the BIEF, are hard at work putting the wheels into motion. Everything must be thought out to the finest detail, and everyone in eventing and show jumping owes those who organise it all a great deal. The people behind the scenes do not step up on a podium to receive gold medals, but they certainly deserve them for effort.

Even as you read this chapter someone, somewhere in Britain, is fund raising on behalf of our equestrians, and each pound they secure helps our riders to move nearer their objectives.

One lady who is employed full-time on fund raising is Bridget Jennings, who works from an office in 35 Belgrave Square – and, on many occasions, continues her work when she goes home. She is completely dedicated to her task, but admits that finding money is never easy. 'It was particularly difficult with the Aintree fund going on,' she said, 'but we understood their problems and carried on the best way we could. After all, our teams have got to go abroad before the Olympics, and to the Games themselves, and we have to pay for it. Basically, it is an ongoing situation, and all sorts of ideas to raise money are put up at committee meetings. We put the best ones into action and go on from there.

'What we try to do, if we are running a show, or something else, is to get it sponsored, so that all the proceeds can then go into the fund. We stage raffles, dances, in fact anything that will raise money from, say, £1000 to £20,000. It all helps. I am a full-time employee and there are eleven Committee members, including the chairman, Roger Palmer.'

Every four years, from now into the foreseeable future, Britain will be sending equestrian teams to the Olympic Games – who knows, one day we might actually win an individual show-jumping gold medal! It is really just a matter of time and, indeed, money. To make it possible for our equestrians to go to any Olympics costs between £100,000 and £150,000, so we shall always need a steady supply of funds.

Instead of receiving massive state help, as some countries do – particularly the Eastern Bloc nations whose governments pay for everything – our people have to work hard at supplying that money themselves apart, that is, from the help they gratefully receive from

*Bridget Jennings – one of the top fund raisers*

the Sports Council. It takes a lot of organising and much dedication from those directly involved with the task of approaching individuals or companies and asking them for financial support. It has to be remembered that the equestrian authorities are not the only ones who are fund raising – there are many others who think their needs are as great, if not greater, than those of the horse world. Everything, however, has its place and fortunately there are enough people in Britain who consider that it is important to try to win Olympic medals, gold or otherwise.

And, as long as they keep coming forward with their donations, Britain can continue the battle of finding, preparing and sending our equestrian teams to all parts of the globe to gain experience before tackling the Olympics.

# 19
# Stars of the Past

Any sport is only as popular as the individuals taking part, but eventing has two major advantages over most others: it has horses as well as humans to become public favourites, and the sport lends itself to heroic deeds. It was designed originally as a testing ground for officers' chargers, and therefore had truly to reflect a horse's stamina and courage: in modern times it has become much modified, but still the intrinsic nature of the three-day event provokes some public accusation of being too demanding. If a man drains himself to the uttermost running in a marathon, he is a hero; if, like Bill Roycroft in the Rome Olympics, he leaves his hospital bed with a broken shoulder to ride in the final show-jumping phase, and helps his team win the gold medal, that is heroism too. Ask too much of a horse, and the outrage is immediate. How much is too much? Sometimes the answer is obvious, often it is a matter of opinion, but most of the equine heroes have been those who made the whole thing look easy.

Any arbitrary list of horses who have made eventing history is bound to have notable omissions, but surely an obvious claimant to lead the way is the only horse ever to have won two individual Olympic gold medals, in 1928 and 1932, Marcroix, ridden for the Netherlands by Charles Ferdinand Pahud de Mortanges, then a lieutenant in the Dutch Hussars. Mortanges already had a team gold medal to his credit, for he rode Johnny Walker in the Dutch team that won in Paris in 1924, finishing fourth individually.

Marcroix was not, in fact, a Dutch horse, but was bred in France, in May 1919 at Corbary, near Charolles,

and was an Anglo-Normand. He was by the English Thoroughbred Marsan out of a half-bred mare Coquet, and was originally called Tenor. He had four white socks, which used to be taken as a sure sign of a horse to 'go without', but his record refutes such old wives' tales. Bred by the Marquis de Croy, he was ridden in France by Captain Labouchère, a talented cross-country rider, before being bought by Mortanges to ride in the 1928 Games, held in Amsterdam.

It was a desperately close-run finish, with Mortanges and Marcroix lagging behind compatriot Captain Gerard de Kruyff on Va-t-en in the dressage but overtaking them in the speed and endurance phase to win by less than three points, 1969.82 to 1967.26. Lieutenant Voort van Zijp and Silver Piece, individual winners in Paris, were fourth, giving the Netherlands a decisive team victory.

Only four teams travelled to Los Angeles for the 1932 Games, and the Dutch went the whole way by boat, taking nearly a month for the journey. To keep the horses fit they rigged up a most ingenious device, like the moving 'walkway' belts at some airports; this treadmill was set at a slight slope and each horse in the Dutch team was given up to an hour's exercise on this every day. It may not have been very exciting for them, but it did its job; they were on full rations all the way and landed in California ready to go straight into strong work, and were fully fit for the event in just two weeks. The Dutch team were runners-up this time, to the United States, but Mortanges and Marcroix won their second gold, again by a narrow margin, from the

American Lieutenant Earl Thomson, on Jenny Camp. Perhaps Marcroix was lucky, for Jenny Camp cleared the water jump in the show jumping but a hind foot slipped back into it, at a cost of ten penalty points, and still finished only just over two points behind.

Marcroix survived until the Second World War, and was used during it as a draft horse under the German occupation. General Mortanges died in 1971.

Earl Thomson and Jenny Camp's run of near misses dogged them into the Berlin Olympics in 1936, when they could so easily have dented the German domination that took all six equestrian gold medals. Jenny Camp, an Army horse from birth, having been bred in 1926 on a remount station in Virginia, and Captain Thomson again took the silver, behind Ludwig Stubbendorf on Nurmi, after being penalised for a refusal, and losing much time, across country even though they were stopped by an official because there was a rider in the ditch ahead of them. And Stubbendorf went undisqualified although he failed to make the weight: but for a non-German to win in Berlin, 1936, was like trying to beat an American boxer on his home ground – 'you have to knock them out to win on points'.

Jenny Camp retired to stud after that, but Thomson returned to the Olympic fray after the war, and in London in 1948 rode in both the three-day event, when the United States took the team gold, and in the dressage, in which they finished second to France. There was much less specialisation in those days than there is now: Mexico's Humberto Marilés, who won the show-jumping gold at those Games, also rode in the event and finished twelfth.

Until after the Second World War eventing, like all international equestrian sport, was a purely military matter, but then the floodgates were opened to civilians, of whom pride of place should perhaps go to Englishman John Shedden on an American-bred horse, Golden Willow, winners of the first Badminton in 1949. Shedden was already then a well-established trainer, and this new sport – new at least as far as the British as a whole were concerned – was something which immediately attracted him. Golden Willow, who belonged to American Mrs Kidston, was out of a top-rate Irish hunter, Pussy Willow, who, together with his owner's other horses, was sent back to her United States home at the outbreak of the war. In Virginia she was mated with Cloth of Gold, a son of Sir Galahad III, one of America's greatest racehorses, and the produce was Golden Willow, who came to England, to Shedden's Cotswold stable, as a five-year-old.

Golden Willow combined a superb temperament with, once he was in action, tremendous power, and

Shedden asked Mrs Kidston if he could train the horse for three-day events. There were, in the late 1940s, no one-day horse trials as there are now, in which to give a horse experience, building him up to such a test as Badminton. There was just Badminton. Now, of course, there are strict qualifications to ensure that a horse cannot compete there until he is ready to do so, but for the inauguration of what has become the world's greatest three-day event the only qualifications were that the riders should be British – this did not last long, but it was, after all, originally designed to give British riders the chance to develop to Olympic standard – were over seventeen years old, and that the horses were not over ten years. Golden Willow was some way behind Tony Collings and Remus in the dressage, a phase to which his explosive temperament was not ideally suited, but galloped way into the lead in the cross-country and stayed there.

Tony Collings, another great and immediate enthusiast for eventing, had his turn the following spring, again on Remus, when Shedden was second with Kingpin and fifth on Golden Willow.

The Queen, whose close association with Badminton three-day event has undoubtedly played a huge part in its popularity, was involved right from the early days, and bought Countryman III from Bertie Hill. Hill continued to ride him, including in the team that won Britain's first Olympic gold, at Stockholm in 1956. They were fourth in the next year's Badminton, but Her Majesty had to wait until 1974, when her son-in-law Mark Phillips won on Columbus, for her first victory there.

Frank Weldon, who took the individual bronze medal in Stockholm – the first British rider to win an individual medal – and his Kilbarry were, by any reckoning, one of the great combinations of the sport. To the increasing number of British enthusiasts Kilbarry was to eventing what Harry Llewellyn's Foxhunter was to show jumping.

Kilbarry was bred in Ireland in 1946, by Malbrouck out of a mare by Heligoland, a big bay standing 16.3 hands high, and was bought as a five-year-old by the then Major Weldon from a Nottinghamshire farmer to go racing. That was Weldon's great passion: he won his first point-to-point in 1935, his last twenty-four years later and the Royal Artillery Gold Cup in 1956 and 1957. He was CO of the King's Troop, RHA, in 1951 when someone mentioned Badminton three-day event to him; he knew nothing of it at the time, but when he found out, he decided it would be good exercise for his young officers. He and two others went to Badminton in 1952; the others got round but Weldon finished up in

Above: *Frank Weldon and the legendary Kilbarry during the show-jumping phase of the Stockholm Olympics*

Right: *Margaret Hough, creating history as the first woman to win the Badminton Horse Trials, on Bambi V, in 1954*

hospital, and decided that if he was to do any good at it would have to take it more seriously.

Kilbarry's racing career was cut short when he was a victim of a coughing epidemic that swept through the St John's Wood stables, and never quite recovered. He was Hobdayed, and although he ran in and won a point-to-point in the spring of 1953 he then went eventing; he won a one-day trial at Stowell Park, and was a last-minute choice for the British team for the inaugural European Championships, which were to take place at Badminton. In this his first three-day event he finished second, and he and Weldon were second at Badminton again the next year, when they should have won but

for a timing mistake in the steeplechase; they travelled to Basle, Switzerland, and finished second to Bertie Hill and Crispin in the European Championships, with Lawrence Rook and Starlight XV giving the British team a clean sweep.

In 1955 Weldon and Kilbarry won every competition they entered, including the European Championships at Windsor – there was no Badminton that year – and the three-day event at Harewood, Yorkshire, one-day events and hunter trials, show jumping and officer's charger classes. They won their Olympic bronze, and team gold, in 1956, but on 13 April 1957 Kilbarry was killed when he broke his neck in a fall at a simple fence

at the Cottesbrooke one-day event. A tragic end to a career during which he dominated the sport more than any other horse has ever done.

Margaret Hough was the first woman to win Badminton, on Bambi V in 1954. Since then the fair sex has proved more than able to match their male rivals, and Sheila Willcox is still the only rider so far to have won Badminton three times in succession, on High and Mighty in 1957 and 1958, and on Airs and Graces in 1959. High and Mighty, bred in Ireland by a thoroughbred out of an Arab-Highland cross mare, was brought over to England by his breeder and bought by Sheila as a seven-year-old. He soon nearly came to a sticky end,

when he fell into a muddy creek near Sheila's Lancashire home and had almost disappeared before he was hauled out by a tractor: he never much liked jumping water after that, but was brilliantly trained and had the utmost trust in his rider.

Their first three-day event was the 1955 European Championships at Windsor, when they finished thirteenth and were then fourth behind Kilbarry at Harewood. Based on these performances they were chosen for the team for an international event in Turin – which had a bigger entry than the official European Championships – and won it. Next year they had a pulsating struggle with Weldon and Kilbarry at Badminton before

*Sheila Willcox one of the all-time greats on High and Mighty galloping through the water jump at Badminton in 1957*

being narrowly beaten into second place and, because women were still not allowed in the Olympic Games, Sheila was asked to place High and Mighty at the disposal of the selectors for someone else to ride. She resisted as long as possible, convinced that the horse would not go well for another, but finally agreed to sell him to Mr Ted Marsh on the understanding that she would have the ride again after the Games. But High and Mighty did not get on with his new rider, and then went lame and could not compete anyway; Chris Collins, the present chairman of the British Selectors, was put in

a similar situation many years later, and refused, and it is his firm policy never to try to persuade riders to lend their horses for another rider in any team.

The horse went back to Sheila; in 1957 they won Badminton and the European Championships, and repeated their Badminton success in 1958, upon which Sheila Willcox retired him from eventing, and produced Airs and Graces to complete a hat-trick in 1959. Nearly a decade later she won Burghley on Fair and Square, whose only, unplanned, foal was Lucinda Prior-Palmer's Be Fair. A tragic accident cut short Sheila's career but she fought back with typical courage and, after being told she might never walk again, later rode in dressage competitions.

With Sheila Willcox and High and Mighty in that

victorious 1957 team was Derek Allhusen on Laurien, whose family story is one of the most romantic in eventing. Allhusen, then a major in the 9th Lancers, was stationed in northern Italy, near Padua, at the end of the war when he heard that some of the horses being 'demobilised' at a nearby transport corps were worth looking at. He went, saw them and bought a German-bred mare who had been captured by the British 8th Army; he gave just £50 for her, including her transport back to England. She was a good show jumper and Allhusen, who had competed for Britain in the pentathlon at the 1948 Winter Olympics in St Moritz, finishing sixth, was chosen for the squad for a pentathlon at the same year's summer Games in London.

While training just before the event Laura, as she was now called, went lame, and the horse Derek rode as a substitute fell, rolled on him and dislocated his shoulder. He had to be left out of the team, and Laura went to stud, covered by Davy Jones who, but for a broken rein, would surely have won the 1936 Grand National. Their progeny was Laurien, who as well as being in the 1957 team was second to High and Mighty at Badminton, 1957; fourth there the next year; took an individual bronze and team silver at the European Championships of 1959; and was twice leading prizewinner in Britain. Twelve years later her son Laurieston, by Happy Monarch, was ridden by Richard Meade to win the individual and a team gold medal in the Munich Olympics. Derek Allhusen had himself taken an individual silver and team gold four years before that on Lochinvar at the Mexico Games, but decided to give way to the younger man in Munich.

Happy Monarch was the sire also of the greatest of all event horses, who went on to be a brilliant show jumper and could, according to one prominent racehorse trainer, have won the Grand National had he been a racehorse – Merely-a-Monarch. Coincidentally it was Derek Allhusen who was instrumental in Anneli Drummond-Hay, who rode him to his most famous victories, buying 'Monarch'. Indeed, it was Allhusen who first bought him from his Yorkshire breeder for just £300, with the proviso that Anneli should have him if and when she wanted, for the same price, and Derek's wife, Claude, who named him so aptly. Merely-a-Monarch's dam, Highland Fling, was descended from a Highland pony and, at 14.3 hands high, was little more than a pony herself, but Monarch was a magnificent horse nearly two hands higher, and one season's hunting was all Anneli needed to realise just what a horse he was.

Monarch began his meteoric rise to fame as a five-year-old, in 1960, when he was simultaneously competing in one-day trials and show jumping, in which he won a regional final of the Foxhunter Championship and came fourth in the final at the Horse of the Year Show, where he also won the combined training competition. In the following spring he had a training gallop at a racing stable near to where Anneli lived that was so impressive it nearly changed his career to that of racehorse; but she kept him for eventing, won a few minor competitions and turned the inaugural running of the Burghley three-day event that autumn into a procession. Just a few months later they galloped away with Badminton and then, because women were still unable to ride in Olympic three-day events, Anneli took him show jumping. Just a few weeks after Badminton they won the historic Imperial Cup at the Royal International Horse Show at the White City – but then Monarch's story took on a sour note.

He was sold to Robert Hanson, on the understanding that Anneli should continue to ride him; but early in 1964, Olympic year, Monarch lost form and Mr Hanson gave the ride to David Broome. It did not work, Monarch missed the Tokyo Games – where, ironically, women were at last allowed to compete in three-day events – and after litigation, and with the help of Lieutenant Colonel Tom Greenhalgh, Merely-a-Monarch was returned to Anneli, and remained their joint property until he died in 1980. Although he went back briefly into horse trials, and won at Crookham, show jumping was now his game, and he helped his rider win the 1968 European Championship and finish third for the World title in 1970, when they also won the classic Queen Elizabeth II Cup and the Madrid Grand Prix.

Early in the 1960s a team – or to be exact a collection of individuals – came from Australia to challenge the riders from the northern hemisphere in this most exacting of sports. Australian riders actually made their Olympic three-day event debut at Stockholm in 1956 – a fair swap, because the Games themselves were being held in Melbourne, but not the equestrian events, because of Australian quarantine regulations. They only just missed the medals, finishing fourth as a team, and learned enough to whet their appetites for future forays. Laurie Morgan was left out of the Stockholm team even though he and Gold Ross finished fourth, behind Kilbarry, at Badminton in 1955, and were third there, to Kilbarry and High and Mighty, in 1956. But he came back as part of the team for the 1960 Games with Salad Days, who must rank, together with Bill Roycroft's Our Solo – another in that same side – as two of the best horses ever to come out of Australia. At least until Regal Realm fell into Lucinda Green's hands!

Bill Roycroft has become a legend in the sport that he did not take up until he was forty-two years old, four years before Rome. A farmer in Victoria, 6 foot tall, lean and tough, he show jumped and played polocrosse – a mixture of polo and lacrosse – until he bought Our Solo, who stood just 15 hands high, for £50. Our Solo, a thoroughbred, had been bred for pony racing but grew 2 in too high; an intelligent little horse who performed circus tricks for fun, was good-looking enough to win hack classes, and had the power and stamina for eventing. Solo worked at rounding up

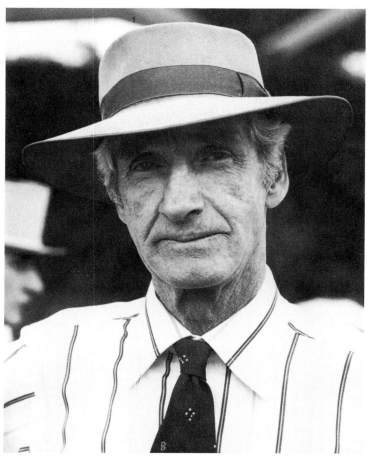

*Bill Roycroft, one of the best international riders that Australia has ever produced*

stock, too, jumping everything in sight as he did so. Roycroft, who had ridden all his life, had his biggest problem with dressage, but taught himself, with the aid of Henry Wynmalen's books, well enough to get Our Solo into second place in their first three-day event, in Melbourne in 1958: they were second there twelve months later, and won the events at Sydney and Gawler.

With them in the team for the Rome Olympics, and

a preliminary outing at Badminton, were Morgan and Salad Days, Brian Crago, who had been in the Stockholm team and now lives in England, on Sabre, and Neale Lavis with Mirrabooka. They took Badminton by storm, Our Solo first, Salad Days second and Mirrabooka fourth, and then won the dramatic three-day event at Rome that is described in detail in the chapter on the Olympics. Little Our Solo was as tough as his rider, and after Rome was second in Sydney and won the Pony Club Championship for Bill's son, Barry.

Our Solo retired to live out his days as a stock horse, but Bill Roycroft has made many welcome returns to Europe and in 1965 had three rides at Badminton, finishing second and sixth on Eldorado and Stoney Crossing in the major competition and second on Avatar in Little Badminton (for a few years Badminton was run in two sections); Bill went on to ride Stoney Crossing into third place in the Cheltenham Gold Cup, Britain's most important steeplechase, and, together with son Barry, was in Australia's show-jumping team which finished third in the Nations Cups in London and Dublin. Bill and another son, Wayne, were also in the team that took bronze medals in the Mexico and Montreal Olympic Games.

Laurie Morgan and Bill Roycroft had two major attributes in common: they were both in their forties when they started eventing, and both loved racing. Morgan based himself in Gloucestershire for a while and had a highly successful campaign in hunter chases with College Master, while Salad Days, by Hunters Moon, was a useful racehorse on the flat before Morgan bought him and turned his attention to eventing. They won twice in Australia before coming to Europe for the Rome Olympics, where they took the individual gold as well as leading their team to victory.

Laurie Morgan was determined to take Badminton's Whitbread Trophy home with him as well, but Salad Days was running in a hunter chase only ten days before the 1961 event, and then Morgan discovered, only the day before the event started, that he had learned the wrong dressage test. But if it was not as good a start as they intended, Salad Days was close enough at the end of the first phase for his tremendous cross-country ability to take him to victory, with only the veteran Irishman Harry Freeman-Jackson on St Finnbarr able to make any sort of a challenge.

Surprisingly, Ireland, home of superb cross-country horses, has produced few world stars to run under their own flag, but such a one was Major Eddie Boylan's Durlas Eile. Bred in County Tipperary, Durlas Eile had a high-class racing pedigree but not quite the speed to go with it; but if it was not enough for the racecourse,

*Australian Laurie Morgan on Salad Days, safely negotiating a fence at the Rome Olympics, 1960*

he could go across country like an express train, seemingly inexhaustible. He was sold to the Irish Army as a five-year-old, and his breeder, Father McSweeney, eagerly wanted to buy him back, but his very eagerness intrigued the then chairman of the Irish Selection Committee, Thady Ryan, who had already heard of the horse from Major Boylan. Ryan talked Boylan into buying him.

Eddie had been on the fringe of Olympic selection before, and always something prevented it. Alas, even with such a horse as Durlas Eile, his greatest ambition remained unfulfilled; but they did lead the way in one of the Irish team's most purple patches, which included the first-ever World Championships, at Burghley in 1966, and the individual European Championship at Punchestown the next season. Rider and horse joined forces in July 1964, just too late for the Tokyo Games; but they were fourth at Burghley that autumn and led from start to finish at Badminton, 1965. Show jumping was Durlas Eile's major flaw – his dressage was a dream and his cross-country no less so – and this dropped them behind the Russians in the European Champion-

ships of 1965 in Moscow. It left Eddie and his horse only fourth individually in the World Championships as well, and cost them Badminton, 1967, but on home ground for that year's European they gave one of the best dressage tests seen in a three-day event, and came home alone. But Eddie had an offer from a Canadian – £19,000, a record price then for an eventer – that he could not refuse, and with it went a certain place in the team for Mexico.

Strange that some of the best of all eventing horses have failed to win Olympic medals: Durlas Eile and Merely-a-Monarch, and even Cornishman V, fourth in Mexico, fourth in Munich, missed individual honours, but at least he won team gold medals in both. Bred in Cornwall and bought by Brigadier Michael Gordon-Watson as a hunter, Cornishman became rather by chance an event horse for daughter Mary when her regular pony was taken over by her brother. Cornishman was no pony: huge and long-striding, he gave his young, slightly-built rider little help to start with, but trainer Dick Stillwell helped them, as he has so many others, to weld together into a partnership. Cornishman remained always highly-strung, a horse who knew himself to be a champion and was not inclined to concentrate too hard except when it really mattered.

He and Mary won their first three-day event, at Tidworth, but a desperately bad cough kept them out of action for most of the rest of the season, and although they were allowed to go *hors concours* round Badminton, 1968 – because of the cough they had not been able to qualify – it was a round which started superbly and ended in disappointment when Cornishman resolutely stopped at the last fence but one, a coffin, the sort of fence he never much cared for. Mary said afterwards, 'The selectors thought he was impressive – but did not think much of me.' He was turned out, with Burghley in view, for no one regarded him as a serious hope for that autumn's Mexico Olympics, and then taken, half-fit, to Wembley for the working hunter class, where he tripped over a fence too small to notice and gave Mary a broken leg.

While she was laid up, Britain's potential Olympic horses fell, one by one, by the wayside, and Richard Meade ended up being given Cornishman to ride in Mexico. In terrible stormy conditions they finished fourth, and the team won. Cornishman was reunited with his owner's daughter in 1969, but the Selectors were far from convinced that Mary was able to do him

*Major Eddie Boylan leaping into action with his brilliant horse Durlas Eile*

justice, and they were chosen only as individuals for the European Championships. Over what many regarded as one of the biggest championship courses ever, they put those selectorial doubts to rest, and twelve months later, over an even more awe-inspiring course at Punchestown, added the World title; so there was no doubting their rightful place in the Munich Olympic side, when once again 'Corny' missed an individual medal by just one place.

Without doubt the rider who has done most to bring three-day eventing to the public attention is Princess Anne. At first most people, if they knew she did it at all, would dismiss the whole thing as the Queen's daughter enjoying herself playing at horse trials; but Princess Anne did not take long to show those who thought along those lines how wrong they were. She made her debut on Purple Star, belonging to the Crown Equerry, Colonel (now Sir) John Miller, but it was her partnership with Doublet that took her to the top. Doublet was no high-priced horse but was bred by the Queen, by the Argentine Triple Crown winner Doubtless out of a pony mare, Swaté, and Princess Anne, trained by Alison Oliver, brought him up through the horse trials ranks. Just five months after their first venture at Badminton, in 1971, where they finished fifth, they won the European Championship at Burghley. Now the world had to take notice, and four years later Princess Anne took the European silver medal behind Lucinda Prior-Palmer, riding the ex-show jumper Goodwill, her partner in the Montreal Olympics. Since having her two children Princess Anne's horse trials activities have mostly been on a lesser scale, but the mark she made is indelible.

The United States, winners of the team gold at the London Olympics in 1948, had to wait until 1974 for their next global triumph, when they won the team World Championship at Burghley, and Bruce Davidson with Irish Cap became the first winner from the States of the individual title. Davidson, a New Englander, was just twenty-three when he and Irish Cap took the Championship – which he was to repeat four years later on Might Tango. His life has always revolved around horses: hunting in his early teens, captain of riding at school, show jumping, eventing, hunter trials – always riding, always competitive – and in 1969 he decided to try for one of the international trials the US Equestrian Team runs regularly to find up-and-coming riders. He went to the USET headquarters at Gladstone, and stayed for three years.

That was where he met Irish Cap, who had been imported unbroken from Ireland and was then being ridden by a girl who could not handle him. Bruce 'made' Irish Cap and likes nothing better than educating young horses. He was in the silver-medal team at the Munich Olympics on Plain Sailing, who finished eighth, and prepared for his attempt at the World title at Burghley by bringing Irish Cap over for the spring season in Britain, finishing third to Mark Phillips and Columbus at Badminton. Whether they would have reversed placings in the World Championships had Columbus not slipped a ligament from his hock as he finished the cross-country at Burghley must forever be in doubt, but with Columbus out of the way Bruce and Irish Cap, with his team mate and captain Mike Plumb a close second on Good Mixture, at last put the USA in front again after years of finishing second.

They stayed there for the Montreal Olympics, with Tad Coffin taking the gold on Ballycor and Plumb second again, this time with Better and Better; and then, in the stifling heat and humidity of Lexington, 1978, Davidson retained his World title, even though his grey Might Tango, like many of the other horses who took part, never had the same sparkle again.

Lucinda Green and Regal Realm wrested their World title from them in 1982, a story which has been related elsewhere in the book. The whole of this book, and more, would have been needed to mention all of the past stars of eventing but these have been some who have brought the sport its most golden moments.

# 20
# Pen Pictures

## Princess Anne (Great Britain)

Princess Anne (15.8.50) made rapid headway as a horse trials rider, at first with Colonel Sir John Miller's Purple Star, and then on Doublet, a brilliant chestnut owned and bred by the Queen. The first time they went to Badminton, in 1971, they were fifth, and in September of the same year they won the European Championship at Burghley. A leg injury kept Doublet out of the Munich Olympic team, and he had to be put down after breaking a leg while exercising at home in 1973. There was worldwide interest when the Princess went to Kiev, in the Soviet Union, that year to defend her European title, riding the former show jumper Goodwill, but their defence ended at the now notorious second fence. They were twelfth in the 1974 World Championships, and took the silver medal in the 1975 European, in Luhmühlen, behind Lucinda Prior-Palmer and Be Fair. They fell but still finished (in twenty-fourth place) in the Montreal Olympics. Princess Anne was out of competition in 1977 when her son, Peter, was born, and retired Goodwill in 1978. Her second child, daughter Zara, was born in 1981, and recently the Princess has confined her attention to novice competitions.

*On the bridle and going well, Princess Anne with Goodwill, the horse she rode in the Montreal Olympics*

## Elizabeth Ashton (Canada)

Elizabeth Ashton (1951) was born in England but lives in Ontario and has combined horse trials and show jumping with considerable success, although eventing is now her main interest. She had her first international jumping success in Washington, at the age of 17, and in 1972 was leading jumping rider in Washington and Toronto and third in the Canadian national three-day event championship. In 1975 she was in the team that won a silver medal in the Pan American Games, was in Canada's team at the Montreal Olympics and captained the team that won the World Championships in 1978 in Lexington. She and Sunrise were eleventh individually, and seventeenth in Fontainebleau in 1980. She is director of equine studies at a Toronto college.

## Rachel Bayliss (Great Britain)

Rachel Bayliss (28.4.50) was considered a one-day horse trials specialist until she and her great and consistent Gurgle the Greek finished second at Burghley in 1978. Five years earlier Gurgle had caused a sensation, and a rule change, by sliding under a tree-trunk over a ditch at Badminton instead of jumping over it. In 1979 Miss Bayliss and Gurgle were selected as individuals for the European Championships in Luhmühlen, and took the silver medal behind Nils Haagensen, after which Mystic Minstrel took over as her main three-day-event horse. Their dressage almost always left them leaders after the first phase, including at Fontainebleau – dressage is Miss Bayliss' long-term aim when she gives up eventing – though the cross-country has sometimes posed problems. In 1982 they finished third at Badminton and, after again leading the dressage, were twenty-second in the World Championships after an unfortunate stop. But their moment finally came in the 1983 European Championships: originally chosen only as non-travelling reserves they came into the squad after accidents to other horses, were not quite as good as usual in the dressage, but went superbly across country to go into the lead, and stayed there to become the new European Champions.

*The smile says it all – Rachel Bayliss after winning the European Championships at Frauenfeld, 1983*

# Mervyn Bennett (Australia)

Mervyn Bennett (7.9.44), from Nowra, New South Wales, may be known in Britain mainly as the man who sold Lucinda Green her World Champion horse Regal Realm, but he is a successful Olympic rider in his own right. An apprentice plumber when he left school at fifteen, he acquired his own business two years later and has been building it up ever since. But horses have gone side by side with this; he started riding at twelve, was in the NSW team at the Inter-Pacific Pony Club one-day event at seventeen, and in 1974 captained the first Australian three-day event team to go to New Zealand, where they won. Selected for the Montreal Olympics, his best horse broke down and he had to ride the six-year-old Regal Reign, but finished twelfth and helped his team take the bronze medal. He started riding Regal Realm, bred and part-owned by Sir Alec Cresswick, in 1977, and took him and Regal Reign to Fontainebleau for the 1980 Festival, where he rode Regal Reign to finish sixth individually, with the team again third. He finished thirtieth, again on Regal Reign, in the 1982 World Championships, won, of course, by Lucinda on Regal Realm.

*Merv Bennett takes time out to relax with his wife Anne. Bennett used to ride Regal Realm, the horse on which Lucinda Green won the World title and Badminton for a record fifth time in 1983*

# Sue Benson (Great Britain)

Sue Benson (4.8.51), born in Surrey and living since her marriage in 1979 in Wiltshire, has been a regular and successful member of the British team. As Sue Hatherley she had an unfortunate start to her championship career in the Europeans of 1975 at Luhmühlen, when she and Harley had a fall in the show jumping which dropped Britain from first to second place, behind the USSR. Her best horse so far has been Monacle, with whom she was second at Badminton in 1979, and was later in the European Championship team that took a silver medal, finishing fourth individually. Then she rode Gemma Jay in the team that regained the European title at Horsens in 1981; but she fell and broke a collarbone before the 1982 World Championships, and Gemma Jay was sold in 1983.

# Herbert Blöcker (West Germany)

Herbert Blöcker (1.1.43), a farmer from Elmshorn, came nearest to an individual gold medal when he and Albrant were just edged out of it by the Soviet rider Alexander Evdokimov in the European Championships at Kiev, but his team won the gold there. He and Albrant were also in the teams that won a silver at the Montreal Olympics, a bronze in the 1974 World Championships at Burghley, and a bronze in the 1975 European Championships. On Ladad he finished equal thirteenth in the 1982 World Championships, when the German team was second to Britain.

*Germany's Herbert Blöcker with Albrant at the World Championships in Lexington, 1978*

# Jacek Bobik (Poland)

Jacek Bobik (3.12.60), a student of German philology from Racula, has been one of Poland's most consistent three-day-event riders in the last three years. He rode Koper in the team that finished third in the European Young Riders' Championships in 1981 and, with the same horse, was fourth individually and in the second-placed team at the international event in Waldorf, West Germany, and was third individually and in the winning team at Heide-Kalmthout, Belgium, both in 1982. Bobik and Koper were twenty-ninth in the World Championships, 1982, when the team came in fifth. In 1983 he was in the team that finished second at Waldorf, on Optyk.

## Goran Breisner (Sweden)

Goran Breisner (1.7.54) a member of the team that won the 1983 European Championship, was born in Malmö but has lived in England since 1978, based at the successful Oxfordshire stable of fellow-Swede Lars Sederholm. He first went there seven years earlier, and also spent some time in Ireland. His best horse has been Ultimus – owned jointly by Breisner and Sederholm – who was very fast across country. They were third at Badminton in 1980, fourth in 1981, tenth in 1982 and sixth in 1983. They have been frustrated in their Championship attempts: Ultimus lamed himself just before the 1981 Europeans and had a chill prior to the World Championships in 1982, but they helped Sweden win the unofficial team championship at Boekelo, Holland, that autumn, and were third individually. In Frauenfeld in 1983 they helped pull off a surprise but deserved win for Sweden in the European Championships, with Britain second, and finished fourth individually, the only combination to complete the speed and endurance phase without adding to their dressage score. Sadly, just a couple of weeks later, Ultimus broke a leg while turned out in a field at home in Oxfordshire and had to be put down.

*Down in the forest – Goran Breisner on the ill-fated Ultimus. The horse was later put down after injuring itself in a field*

# Anna Casagrande (Italy)

Anna Casagrande (26.5.58) was born in Milan, only began riding when she was fourteen, and was a member of the Italian team in the European Junior Championships in 1976. Later the same year she and the Irish-bred Daleye were fifteenth in the Alpine Championships at Frauenfeld. She has been a frequent visitor to Britain, and in 1978 she rode Daleye to take third place at Burghley. The following year they were members of the Italian team that finished fourth in the European Championship, and were twenty-third individually. They were members of the team that went to Moscow for the 1980 Olympics and finished second to the Russians, with an individual seventh place. Just a few weeks later they turned out again for the Fontainebleau Festival, but had a fall early in the cross-country. They failed to finish in the World Championships, 1982.

# Diana Clapham (Great Britain)

Diana Clapham (8.6.57), who was born in Malaysia and now lives in Hampshire, had an unhappy start to her international career when, in the 1974 European Junior Championships in Rome, her horse Spindrift went lame, but 'Tiny' Clapham, as she is universally known, has had better luck in the senior division. Sixth place at Badminton, 1981, on Windjammer earned them a place in the squad that contested the European Championships in Horsens and, as an individual, she finished eighth; in the 1982 World Championships they were tenth. She and Windjammer were in the team that took the silver medal in the 1983 European Championships, finishing sixteenth individually.

*Diana 'Tiny' Clapham sails over the Boat on Windjammer, Badminton, 1981*

# Lorna Clarke (Great Britain)

Lorna Clarke (13.1.44) comes from Scotland, but now lives in Berkshire. She won Burghley in 1967 on Popadom, is one of only two people to ride three horses round Badminton (Australia's Bill Roycroft is the other), something which is now forbidden by international rules, and won the pre-Olympic event in Munich in 1971 on Peer Gynt. She went with the squad to the 1972 Games and was expected to get into the team when Debbie West's Baccarat went lame, but stayed on the sidelines and watched the team take a gold medal. She won Burghley again in 1978 on Greco but broke a leg in a fall with the same horse at Badminton, 1980. In 1982 she was second at Hooge Mierde, Holland, with Danville, who finished fourth at Badminton, 1983. At first picked as reserve for the 1983 European Championships, she and Danville came into the team at the last minute and helped them take the silver medal; despite a fall, which badly damaged Lorna's shoulder, they finished fifteenth individually.

*Lorna Clarke and Danville ploughing a furrow through the water at Badminton in 1983*

# Bruce Davidson (USA)

Bruce Davidson (13.12.49) is the only rider ever to have won the World Three-day Event Championship twice, in 1974 on Irish Cap and 1978 on Might Tango. He rode in the Munich Olympics, aged 23, on Plain Sailing, when the US team was second to Britain, and two years later put carefully-laid plans into action in search of the World title. He brought Irish Cap to Britain in the spring, to acclimatise, and finished third at Badminton; the value of this experience was proved when they beat team-mate Mike Plumb, with Good Mixture, for the individual gold at Burghley, and led their team to gain revenge over Britain for the Munich defeat. His victory gave the US the right to stage the 1978 World Championships, which they did at Lexington, Kentucky, when Davidson and Might Tango had the best of a gruelling event. In between, he was in the team that won gold medals in the Pan American Games in 1975 and the Montreal Olympics. He badly broke a foot in a riding accident in 1979 and was out of action for a year, but rode at Badminton in 1981, and was second there in 1982 on J. J. Babu in preparation for an attempt at a hat-trick of World titles, but in Luhmühlen they finished only fourteenth.

*Picture of content – Bruce Davidson with mare and home-bred foal in Unionville, USA*

# Simon de Jonge (Holland)

Simon de Jonge (25.3.57), a company director, has been one of Holland's most consistent riders for the past four years. In 1979 he was fourth in Hooge Mierde and second in the National Championship at Boekelo: he rode Upper Church in the Fontainebleau Festival in 1980 and was the best from his country, finishing twenty-ninth. He and Miracle finished one place higher in the 1982 World Championships, after finishing eighteenth in the Europeans in 1981.

## Torrance Fleischman (USA)

Torrance Watkins Fleischmann (30.7.49), from Virginia, was an instant success when she came to Britain in 1979 with her attractive skewbald mare Poltroon and finished second at Burghley behind Andrew Hoy, but 1980 was an even better year for them. They won two of the selection trials in the United States, at Blue Ridge and Lexington, and were chosen for the event at Fontainebleau which most riders went to instead of the Moscow Olympics. Poltroon is only a tiny mare, but her supporters, who wore tee-shirts emblazoned 'Pinto Puissance' were not let down when she finished third. Mrs Fleischmann bought Southern Comfort, Mark Todd's 1980 Badminton winner, for the 1982 World Championships, and would have finished eighth but for hitting two show-jumping fences, which dropped them to twenty-first place.

*Torrance Watkins Fleischmann on one of the most colourful horses in eventing, Poltroon*

## David Foster (Ireland)

David Foster (26.3.55) was the leading Irish junior event rider in 1971, 1972 and 1973, and finished second in the Gowran Grange Stakes, the national class at Punchestown, in 1971. In 1974 he was second in the international event at Middleton Park. Captain Foster joined the Army Equitation School in 1975 and won the Ballindenisk three-day event in 1977 and the Gowran Grange in 1978. He was a member of the team that won the European Championships at Luhmühlen in 1979, and he and Inis Meain were sixth individually. He rode the same horse to win the international three-day event at Punches- town in 1980 and was in the team that finished fourth at that year's Fontaine-bleau Festival. Brian MacSweeney had the ride on Inis Meain in the 1981 European Championships, finishing third, and Foster was switched to Cill Morain, who fell and retired in the cross-country.

# Mary Gordon-Watson (Great Britain)

Mary Gordon-Watson (3.4.48), from Dorset, won World and European individual and team gold medals, and an Olympic team gold, on her father's great horse Cornishman V. It might have been two Olympic golds, but she was injured and Richard Meade rode Cornishman in the Mexico Olympics. Miss Gordon-Watson was re-united with Cornishman the following season at Haras du Pin, France, to win the European, and in 1970 was among the few able to cope with a big and difficult course for the World Championships at Punchestown. They only just missed an individual Olympic medal in Munich when they finished fourth, as Cornishman had with Meade in Mexico. Miss Gordon-Watson now trains horses and riders, and is a member of the Horse Trials International Selection Committee.

*Mary Gordon-Watson – a perfect take-off with Speculator III, ridden to victory at Badminton in 1982 by Richard Meade*

# David Green (Great Britain)

David Green (28.2.60) was born in Brisbane, Australia, but took British nationality in December 1983, and lives in England, with his World Champion wife Lucinda. David met Lucinda while she was on a working holiday in Australia in 1979, and they married two years later. He brought horses to England from his homeland, but he has had most success with horses formerly ridden by Lucinda, in particular Botany Bay and Mairangi Bay. He and Botany Bay won the Irish three-day event at Punchestown in 1982, with Lucinda runner-up. On Mairangi Bay he was sixth at Badminton in 1982 – with Lucinda and Regal Realm seventh – but they had a fall across country in the World Championships, finishing forty-third. The three man Australian team was sixth. In Badminton 1983 they were going exceptionally well until they parted company at the Bull Pens. He rode Mairangi Bay to a uniquely close victory over Lucinda on Beagle Bay in the first running of the Gatcombe Horse trials in 1983, when both finished with the same score in the same time and the

judges had to go back to their original good marks in the dressage, which gave David the edge by just one mark. Like Lucinda, David is sponsored by SR Direct Mail.

*David Green taking everything in his stride with Mairangi Bay at Badminton in 1982*

*Happy moment for Lucinda Green, after winning the world title at Luhmühlen in 1982*

# Lucinda Green (Great Britain)

Lucinda Green (7.11.53) first came to the public spotlight when, as Lucinda Prior-Palmer, she won Badminton on Be Fair at the age of 19. They were chosen for the British team for the European Championships in Kiev later in 1973, but she had to wait another two years before she took the European title for the first time, still riding Be Fair, whom her parents had bought her as a fifteenth-birthday present. This was in Luhmühlen where, in 1982, she crowned a magnificent career by taking the World title, on Regal Realm. Mrs Green has

proved herself a true champion by her ability to reach the pinnacles of her sport on a variety of horses. All five of her victories at Badminton have been on different horses: in 1976 she rode Wide Awake (who dropped dead as he was about to complete his second lap of honour); in 1977 she was on George; in 1979 she won with Killaire, and in 1983 with Regal Realm. Riding George she became, in 1977, the only rider to win the European Championship twice, and nearly made it three in 1983, on Regal Realm, who was twentieth after the dressage and pulled up to take the silver medal behind Rachel Bayliss. She was awarded the MBE in 1978, and married Australian three-day-event rider David Green in 1981.

# Peter Green (USA)

Peter Green (31.3.48), from Maryland, made his first appearance in a championship in 1982. After he had finished fourth riding Branchwater in the trial event at Lexington, he was picked as an individual rider for the World Championships in Luhmühlen, and finished eighth.

*Taking the strain, Nils Haagensen and Monaco at Luhmühlen, 1979*

# Nils Haagensen (Denmark)

Nils Haagensen (20.5.55) made his first Olympic appearance as a dressage rider, in the Danish team at the Montreal Olympic Games, and only took up eventing when Monaco's owner asked him to take over the ride. Their elevation to the top of this particular field was meteoric, for just over a year after his first event, Haagensen became European Champion, in 1979. Nils' father, who owns a clothing shop some forty miles from Copenhagen, and is a dressage rider himself, was his son's first tutor, but when he decided to take up horse trials, Nils came to Britain, and was based with Bertie Hill. Haagensen won the first three-day event he rode in, in 1978, on Camicorn, was ninth at Badminton in 1979 and went on to lead from start to finish in the Europeans, at Luhmühlen, 1979. The following year they won the Festival event at Fontainebleau, but Monaco was then retired. Haagensen defended his European title in Horsens in 1981 on a horse he had borrowed only a few weeks earlier and, still looking for a replacement for Monaco, was twenty-third in the 1982 World Championships on Fair Lady.

# Mary Hamilton (New Zealand)

Mary Hamilton (30.10.54), from Hawkes Bay, was one of the squad that made New Zealand's first raid on the World Championships, at Lexington, Kentucky, in 1978. Riding Vladivostok, she retired in the speed and endurance phase, but persevered and was based in the United States until she came to Britain in the autumn of 1981 to ride her home-bred Whist at Burghley. Sadly he failed the first veterinary inspection after knocking a leg. She had better luck at the 1982 World Championships, finishing thirty-ninth on Ben Arthur, and is currently based with Mike and Angela Tucker in Gloucestershire.

*Mary Hamilton of New Zealand going well at Luhmühlen in 1982*

# Jessica Harrington (Ireland)

Jessica Harrington (25.2.47), from County Kildare, is the mother of three children but that has not stopped her carving a notable international eventing career, most recently with the good little mare Amoy. As Jessica Fowler, she was sixth on Ginger Nut in her first European title attempt, at Punchestown, 1967, and was in the team that finished second to Britain. In 1981 she and Amoy were fifth at Badminton and won the Irish international at Punchestown; they were the best from their country, sixteenth in the 1982 World Championships.

*Jessica Harrington and Amoy out of the Lake at Badminton, 1980*

# Dietmar Hogrefe (West Germany)

Dietmar Hogrefe (25.8.62) is one of West Germany's most promising younger event riders. Hogrefe, from Hövelhof, is in the Army; he made his championship debut in the European Juniors, 1980, and finished ninth; in the Young Riders Championship of 1981 he took the individual bronze. He was German champion in 1982 and chosen for their team for the World Championships in Luhmühlen, which took the silver medal behind Britain, with Hogrefe and his nine-year-old Foliant finishing in nineteenth place.

# Jane Holderness-Roddam (Great Britain)

Jane Holderness-Roddam (7.1.48) was the third of the four talented Bullen children, whose mother was both a fine artist and a first-rate horsewoman. Jane won Badminton with her little horse Our Nobby in 1968 and went with him to take a team gold in the Mexico Olympics; both her elder brother Michael and sister Jennie have also ridden in the Olympics, in three-day events and dressage, respectively. Jane, a registered nurse, also won Burghley in 1976, and Badminton two years later on Warrior, owned by American Mrs Suzy Howard, who gave Jane a half-share so that she could compete with the horse for Britain in the 1978 World Championships; later Mrs Howard gave the horse to Jane entirely.

*Jane Holderness-Roddam with Warrior, a great favourite with eventing fans. They are seen here at Badminton in 1980*

# Virginia Holgate (Great Britain)

Virginia Holgate (2.2.55) can almost divide her career into two sections. As a youngster she won the European Junior Championship on Dubonnet in 1973, when the British team also triumphed, and two years later took the pre-Olympic event in Montreal. But in 1977 she had a fall that resulted in her left arm being so badly broken, in more than

*Virginia Holgate is all smiles after winning on Priceless at Burghley, 1983*

twenty places, that there was a possibility it might have to be amputated. She came back bravely on two horses owned by her uncle, Major Rice, and especially with Priceless, on whom she won the Midland Bank Open Championship in 1981 and 1982. On Priceless she made her senior team debut in the 1981 European Championships, and led them to victory, a feat she repeated in the World Championships in 1982, when she was seventh individually. Priceless was ill early in 1983, so Virginia rode Night Cap in the team that took the European Championship silver medal, finishing eighth individually; and then won Burghley on a fully-recovered Priceless.

# Nick Holmes-Smith (Canada)

Nick Holmes-Smith (1960) started eventing when he was ten, and was sixteen when he rode in his first international, a students' competition in Germany, which the Canadians won. The son of a fruit farmer from Oliver, British Columbia, he is also a show-jumping rider. He was a member of the Canadian team that went to the Fontainebleau 'Alternative Olympics' event. In the 1982 World Championships he finished thirty-sixth on Sinnerman, and his team, which had won four years earlier in Lexington, was eighth.

# Andrew Hoy (Australia)

Andrew Hoy (8.2.59) was the first Australian to win Burghley, on Davey in 1979, although two of his compatriots, Bill Roycroft and Laurie Morgan, had scored at Badminton nearly twenty years earlier. Hoy, from New South Wales, took Davey to the 1978 World Championships in Lexington, Kentucky, and brought him on to England, staying at Gatcombe Park as the guest of Mark Phillips and Princess Anne. He stayed until 1980 and was a member of the team that won a bronze medal at the Fontainebleau 'Alternative Olympics',

finishing twenty-fifth. He then returned to Australia, but went to Luhmühlen for the 1982 World Championships and was ninth, the team finishing sixth.

*Australia's Andrew Hoy with his Burghley winner, Davey*

# Mark Ishoy (Canada)

Mark Ishoy (1956) made his first international appearance in 1975, at a student games in West Germany, and within three years was a member of the team that won the World Championships in Lexington, Kentucky. Riding Law and Order, the horse on which earlier the same season he had won the Canadian championship at Jokers Hill, Ishoy, whose brother Neil is also an international, finished eighth individually in the 1978 World Championships, the highest Canadian placing. He was also in the team that contested the Fontainebleau Festival event in 1980. He missed the 1982 World Championships in Luhmühlen.

# Neil Ishoy (Canada)

Neil Ishoy (1952) followed his elder brother Mark into the Canadian national squad after a successful junior career with the Ontario team in 1976 and 1977. He was eighth in the international event held at Lexington, Kentucky, 1979, and ninth there the following year, after which he was chosen, with Mark, for the team for Fontainebleau. He failed to finish there, but was forty-second on L'Esprit in the 1982 World Championships.

# Jan Jonsson (Sweden)

Jan Jonsson (1947) was born in Stockholm and was still in the Swedish Army when he rode Sarajevo to take a bronze individual medal, behind Richard Meade, at the Munich Olympic Games. Although he has been a consistent competitor in international events since then, the nearest he has come to another medal was when fourth on Lyrik at the European Championships in Horsens, 1981; in the 1982 World Championships they had a fall and finished forty-sixth, with their team seventh.

# Horst Karsten (West Germany)

Horst Karsten (1.1.36) won his first championship medal, a bronze, at the 1965 Europeans in Moscow; his only other individual medals have been of the same colour, in the European Championships of 1973 and 1977, both on his grey Sioux, one of the most consistent horses of recent years. He was also in the German teams that triumphed in 1973, were second in 1977 and third in 1969 and 1975 in the Europeans. Karsten, from Delmenhorst, has been five times German national champion; he also won team bronzes in the 1964 Olympics in Tokyo, the 1972 Games in Munich and the World Championships in 1974 at Burghley.

*Poetry in motion, West German Horst Karsten and Sioux at Burghley in 1974*

# Gulam Mohd Khan (India)

Gulam Mohd Khan (11.7.46), a professional soldier and captain in the Indian Army, was a member of the team that won the gold medal in the Asian Games in 1982, and finished second individually, riding Goodwill. He was in the team that won the National Championship in 1980, and won the Individual championship the following season.

*Gulam Khan, professional soldier and a top Indian rider*

# Richard Meade (Great Britain)

Richard Meade (4.12.38) has an outstanding record of Olympic success. He has three gold medals to his credit, for the team wins in Mexico and Munich, and his individual effort on Derek All-husen's home-bred Laurieston, also in Munich. Born in Chepstow, where his parents breed ponies and horses, he made his Olympic debut in Tokyo, 1964, on his own Barberry, with which he had his first major victory, at Burghley, the same year. He rode Cornishman V, in place of the injured Mary Gordon-Watson, in Mexico, and produced another fine piece of Olympic riding when taking Jacob Jones into fourth place in Montreal. He was a member of the team that won the World Championships in 1970 and 1982,

# Jan Lipczynski (Poland)

Jan Lipczynski (15.4.57), a technical engineer from Poznan, has been Polish three-day-event champion twice in the past four years (1980 and 1983) on Elektron, the horse he rode with the Polish team that took a bronze medal at the European Championships in Horsens, in 1981. The team was fifth in the following year's World Championships in Luhmühlen, when he again rode Elektron, finishing twenty-seventh individually. Lipczynski has an especially good record at the Belgian event at Heide-Kalmthout: he won with Elektron in 1980, and with Bastion in 1981, when the Polish team also triumphed. And he was third on Bastion at Amsterdam, also in 1981.

# Brian MacSweeney (Ireland)

Brian MacSweeney (15.4.58) joined the Army Equitation School in 1977 and is an all-round horseman. Lieutenant Mac-Sweeney, from County Dublin, started competing in show jumping and one-day events in 1978, and won the national three-day-event championships at Punchestown on the mare Glenanaar. In 1981 he was runner-up in the national dressage championships, on Gleann Eineach, and was a member of the Irish team at the European Three-day Event Championships in Denmark on Inis Meain, winning the individual bronze medal. He missed the 1982 World Championships as Inis Meain was injured, and in 1983 was concentrating on show jumping.

and the silver in 1974, and that won the European titles in 1967, 1971 and 1981. He won Badminton in 1970 and 1982. He was awarded an OBE in 1974, and in recent years has also played an in-

*Richard Meade, well in control on Wayfarer II, Burghley, 1972*

creasing part in horse trials administration.

## Fiona Moore (Great Britain)

Fiona Moore (20.11.57), daughter of a Hampshire vet, turned from show jumping to horse trials in 1975. She was the season's leading rider under twenty-one the next year and finished eighth at Badminton, 1977, on Drakenburg, which earned them a place on the senior European Championships short-list. Drakenburg was sold in 1978, but she produced Squire's Holt to win the Dutch international event at Boekelo in 1981. In 1983 they finished tenth at Badminton.

## Christian Persson (Sweden)

Christian Persson (1957), a farmer from Skane in the south of Sweden, has been riding since he was three, owned his first pony when he was eight and first tried his hand at competitive show jumping before he turned to horse trials. He has represented his country in several teams, in Holland, Denmark and Germany – where he was in the team that finished second in Luhmühlen in 1981 – before being selected for the European championship in Frauenfeld, Switzerland, in 1983. There he and the then ten-year-old Joel, a Swedish warm-blood, took the individual bronze medal, ahead of compatriot Goran Breisner on Ultimus, and led the team to win the gold medal.

## Mark Phillips (Great Britain)

Mark Phillips (22.9.48) has won Badminton four times – the record until Lucinda Green made it a five-timer in 1983 – and achieved success on a number of different horses. Rock On was his first to reach international recognition, fourth at Burghley, 1967, and Badminton the next spring, after which they were made reserves for the Mexico Olympic team. He rode Chicago in the team that won the World title in 1970 and had his first two Badminton successes in 1971 and 1972 on his aunt Miss Flavia Phillips' Great Ovation. They were in the team that won the European Championships in 1971 and that which took a gold in the Munich Olympics, though they had two falls across country there and so had the discard score. In 1974 he rode Columbus to give the Queen her only success at Badminton, and they were all set to win the World Championship that year when Columbus slipped a tendon from his hock. Captain Phillips, who was in the Queen's Dragoon Guards when he married Princess Anne in November 1973, and now farms at Gatcombe in Gloucestershire, in which county he was born and has always lived, is sponsored by Range Rover, and had his fourth Badminton win for them on Lincoln in 1981.

*Mark Phillips riding high with Lincoln at Badminton in April 1980. He is the only man to have won the Trials four times*

*Maureen Piggott and canine companion at home between events*

# Piotr Piasecki
# (Poland)

Piotr Piasecki (4.9.52), from Wesola, was Polish junior champion in 1969, senior champion in 1976 on Idrys and in 1979 on Kwakier.

# Maureen Piggott
# (Great Britain)

Maureen Piggott (3.5.61), daughter of top jockey Lester, has determinedly made a name for herself as a trials rider, and was in the team which won the first European Young Riders Championships, in 1981, on Asian Princess, and in that which finished second in 1982, on Hong Kong Discoverer. She trained with Alison Oliver until setting up her own stable at Wantage, Berkshire.

# Michael Plumb
# (USA)

Michael Plumb (1940) first rode for the United States event team at the age of nineteen, in 1959, and took part in five consecutive Olympic Games, Rome, Tokyo, Mexico, Munich and Montreal. In the second, third and fourth of these the team was beaten into second place but finally, in Montreal and with Plumb as the riding captain, they won a gold. Plumb, on Better and Better, took the individual silver behind his team-mate Tad Coffin. He also captained the team that won the World Championships in 1974, and the Pan American Games in 1963 and 1967. In the 1974 World Championships, as in Montreal, he was second, this time to Bruce Davidson. In the 1982 World Championships at Luhmühlen, he rode Blue Stone to come in thirty-first.

# Elizabeth Purbrick
# (Great Britain)

Elizabeth Purbrick (16.5.55) was in the British junior team (as Elizabeth Boone) which won the European Junior Championships in 1971 and 1972. Born in Norfolk, but now living in Berkshire, she first made her mark in senior competition on the immensely strong Felday Farmer, who was fourth at Badminton in 1978 and went as an individual to that season's World Championships in Lexington, Kentucky, finishing nineteenth. In the 1979 European Championships they were fifteenth, although she rode most of the cross-country with only one stirrup after the bar of the other had broken. She rode Peter the Great in the team that won the 1981 European Championships, but the horse was badly injured in the spring of 1982 when he escaped from his field and collided with a car.

*Up and over with ease – Lizzie Purbrick on Frederick the Great at Burghley in 1983*

# Helmut Rethemeier (West Germany)

Helmut Rethemeier (8.6.39), a farmer from Vlotho, where he was born, has been a regular member of the West German team since 1975, when he finished fifth in the European Championships. He has won two individual silver medals, and a team silver, but has yet to take a gold. Rethemeier rode the nine-year-old Ladalco, a Holstein, in the 1978 World Championships in Lexington, and finished third. He looked all set for a gold in 1982, when he and Santiago went into the show-jumping phase of the World Championships with a fence in hand over Lucinda Green, but after she had gone clear Santiago had two fences down. He was also second in the European Championships of 1981.

# Sergei Rogozhin (USSR)

Sergei Rogozhin (6.7.56), a builder from Naltchik, and a member of the Russian team since 1974, was in that which won a gold medal in the Moscow Olympics, finishing eleventh individually.

# Anchela Rohof (Holland)

Anchela Rohof (26.2.55), who made her international debut at Siekkrug in 1978 when she finished second and third, had to wait until 1982 for her first international victory when, after coming third at Breda, she won at Hooge Mierde. On the strength of that she and Resolution Bay – a former inmate of Lucinda Green's stable – were chosen for the Dutch team for the World Championships, in which they finished forty-fifth.

# Federico Euro Roman (Italy)

Federico Euro Roman (29.7.52) was born in Trieste and started riding when he was thirteen, taught by his father, an NCO in the Cavalry. He rode in flat races, and began to concentrate on three-day events in 1968; he won the Italian national junior championship the next year, and in 1974 won both the national three-day-event and dressage titles. His first World Championship was in 1974 at Burghley, where he retired. He and Shamrock were ninth in the Montreal Olympics and were in the Italian team that finished fourth. They won the Olympic individual gold medal in Moscow in 1980, on Rossinan, when Italy, Mexico and India were the only non-Iron Curtain countries to take part; the Italian team finished second to the USSR.

# Yuri Salnikov (USSR)

Yuri Salnikov (6.6.50), a teacher from Rostov-on-Don, has been a member of the Soviet team since 1973. He rode Pintset to take an individual bronze and team gold medal at the Moscow Olympics. He and Akoprin were eliminated across country in the 1982 World Championships, when his Soviet team finished last.

# Hansueli Schmutz (Switzerland)

Hansueli Schmutz (1950) was the unexpected winner of the 1981 European Championship on his Dutch-bred Oran. Until only four years earlier Schmutz, who runs a riding school, had concentrated on show jumping, but when he bought Oran as a five-year-old he turned to eventing, and won at Walldorf, in Germany, before his triumph at Horsens. He was trained by ex-Swiss Cavalry officer Ernst Lanz, and led his team to take the silver in Horsens. But the whole Swiss team withdrew from the World Championships in 1982 at Luhmühlen when one of their members, Ernst Baumann, was killed in a fall across country.

*Hansueli Schmutz and Oran, on the way to winning the European Championship at Horsens in 1981*

# Rudiger Schwarz (West Germany)

Rudiger Schwarz (17.5.50) has had his success in international events on the British-bred Power Game. They were in the team in the 1978 World Championships but Power Game got loose while being hosed down, dashed off and injured himself. He recovered in time for the European Championships in Luhmühlen the following year, however, and finished third. They were in the team that finished second in Fontainebleau in 1980, at the 'Alternative Olympics', finishing eleventh individually, and helped Germany take the silver team medal in the 1982 World Championships, when they came in fourth.

# Bishal Singh (India)

Bishal Singh (4.1.43), born in Sanwloda, was a show jumper before he turned to three-day events. Ris Bishal Singh, like all the members of the team that won the Asian Games gold medal, is in the Army, and was the only member of the team who had also ridden in the 1980 Moscow Olympics. In the same year he was in the team that won the Indian national three-day event.

*Bishal Singh, a credit to eventing in India*

# Milkha Singh (India)

Milkha Singh (10.11.47), from Daleki in the Punjabi district of Amritsar, is from a family of agriculturalists and enroled in the President's Bodyguard, the senior regiment of the Indian Army, in 1968. He soon showed evidence of his riding ability, excelled in a nine-month animal management and equitation course and, after taking part in a number of competitions, was sent for advanced equitation training to Italy. Colonel Grignolo was team trainer for the twelve months up to the Asian Games in Delhi, 1982, the first time equestrian events were included. Dafadar Milkha Singh was in the team that won the gold medal.

*Milkha Singh, a dashing figure in Indian eventing*

# Prahalad Singh (India)

Prahalad Singh (21.11.43), born in Hukampura, is probably the only Indian rider to have won a horse trial in Europe, a one-day event in France in 1982. He rode as an individual in the Asian Games in New Delhi, and took the bronze medal on Ranjit.

*Prahalad Singh, a man of pride and talent*

# Raghubir Singh (India)

Raghubir Singh (8.5.51), from Patoda, Rajasthan, won the individual and a team gold medal at the three-day event the first time equestrian events were included in the Asian Games, in Delhi in 1982. Dafadar Raghubir Singh, of the 61st Cavalry, joined the Indian Army in 1969, taking an animal management and equitation course. Riding Shahzada, he was third in the dressage – three of the top four places in that stage were held by Japanese riders, but only the fourth-placed Hidekazu Imai on Happy Times could complete the cross-country course. The Indian team, which had been trained by the Italian Colonel Grignolo for twelve months previously, were supreme across country, eventually filling the first five places, and also winning the team gold.

*Raghubir Singh, individual winner of the Asian Games, 1982*

# Eddy Stibbe
# (Holland)

Eddy Stibbe (1.11.48), whose father is one of the mainstays of eventing in Holland, is probably the most successful rider that country has produced in recent years. He won at Hooge Mierde in 1978 and at Amsterdam in 1980 and 1981; he was Dutch national champion in 1979 and 1980. He and Autumn Affair were forty-first in the 1979 European Championships, and in the Dutch team that finished seventh.

# Clarissa Strachan
# (Great Britain)

Clarissa Strachan (15.8.53), a farmer's daughter from Cullompton, Devon, has been a stalwart of the British team for a decade. She started riding as a four-year-old, competed in her first adult event at sixteen, and made her international debut two years later. Her most consistent horse has been Merry Sovereign and they were in the team that won the European Championships in 1977 and was second in 1979. Although Merry Sovereign was fourteenth in 1982 he showed himself still very much a power when third at the international in Rome in the spring, helping Britain win the unofficial team contest, and then finishing sixth in the World Championships in Luhmühlen. He competed at Badminton seven times consecutively, until and including 1981. Her Delphy Kingfisher was the leading horse in Britain in 1981. Clarissa, who is sponsored by Intercept Alarms, damaged her neck in a bad fall in the autumn of 1983 which prevented her riding in the latter part of the season.

*Clarissa Strachan landing safely with Delphy Kingfisher at Badminton in 1983*

# Karen Straker (Great Britain)

Karen Straker (17.9.64), from York-shire, comes from a family long associated with horses and horse trials; her mother owned and bred, and her brothers rode, George, the horse on which Lucinda Green won her second European Championship. Karen and Running Bear, a former racehorse, won the European Junior Championship in 1982, were by no means disgraced in their first attempt at Badminton when fifteenth in 1983, and took the silver medal at the European Young Riders Championship at Burghley the same year – they would have won with a clear round show jumping – as well as helping the team to take a gold.

*Karen Straker and Running Bear make light of the Wall leading to the Quarry at Badminton, 1983*

# Virginia Strawson (Great Britain)

Virginia Strawson (22.2.63), from Grimsby, has been the most successful of all British young riders in the last two years. She was in the team that won the European Junior Championships in 1980 and was second in 1981, when she won the first of two successive Range Rover training bursaries. She also rode Greek Herb to finish fifth at Burghley in 1981. In 1982 she and the seven-year-old Minsmore won the European Young Riders Championship in Fontainebleau, as well as the National Young Riders Championship at Bramham, and, in her first senior international overseas, won the Dutch three-day event at Boekelo with Sparrow Hawk.

# Miroslaw Szlapka (Poland)

Miroslaw Szlapka (19.9.56) has had his major successes on Erywan. They won the Polish international event at Bialy Bor in 1980 and were the better of only two Polish combinations to compete in the Moscow Olympics that year, finishing sixth. Szlapka was second on Sztorm in the Amsterdam three-day event in 1981 and second also on Jaskier in Bialy Bor, 1981. He and Len were forty-ninth individually, with the team fifth, in the 1982 World Championships.

*Ginny Strawson, a young lady destined for the top in eventing*

# Mark Todd (New Zealand)

Mark Todd (1956) was the first rider from his country to win a major three-day event in the northern hemisphere when he and Southern Comfort triumphed at Badminton in 1980. He had been part of the New Zealand squad at the 1978 World Championships in Kentucky, when he rode Jocasta. He bought Southern Comfort towards the end of 1979 and brought this ex-farm horse to England for the spring season. Soon after winning Badminton, Todd, who was born at Cambridge, in New Zealand's North Island, finished second at Punchestown, Ireland, on Jocasta, but financial considerations forced him to sell both horses before he returned home. Southern Comfort went to the American, Torrance Watkins, but her attempt to win Badminton in 1983 ended before it began, when Southern Comfort failed to pass the first vet test. Todd himself also returned for the 1983 Badminton and, riding Felix Too, an English-owned horse, came ninth.

*Mark Todd from New Zealand being presented with the Whitbread Trophy by the Queen after winning Badminton, 1980, on Southern Comfort*

# Michael Tucker (Great Britain)

Michael Tucker (30.11.44), a Gloucestershire farmer, has long been a pillar of horse trials, on the championship fringe, a situation which might be improved by his home-bred General Bugle, whom he rode into second place at Badminton, 1983, as an eight-year-old. He was second at Burghley, 1969, on Skyborne, third in the pre-Olympic event in Munich, 1971, on Laurieston, whom Richard Meade rode to take two gold medals in the following season's Games, and was seventh in the 1975 European Championships. He is now also a regular commentator at horse trials, and for BBC television.

*Michael Tucker is all smiles, although soaking wet, on General Bugle – a horse with a great future*

# Richard Walker (Great Britain)

Richard Walker (16.8.50) was born in South Africa and came to live in Britain when he was ten. He had a brilliant start to his career with Pasha, on whom he took the European Junior Championship in 1968 and the following season, riding the same horse, beat his elders to become, at 18, the youngest winner of Badminton. That same season he and Pasha were second in the Senior European Championship, in Haras du Pin, and were members of the gold-medal-winning team. After this promising beginning Walker went through a period in the doldrums, concentrating on show jumping rather than eventing, but he came back with a bang to win the Midland Bank Open Championship three years in succession, on Special Constable in 1978 and John O' Gaunt in 1979 and 1980; and he took Burghley twice in three years, on John O' Gaunt in 1980 and Ryan's Cross in 1982. Now living in Oxfordshire, he won the Swedish international event in 1983 and the first running of the Barratt's Scottish Championship on Accumulator.

*Richard Walker, out of the water at Burghley on John O' Gaunt. Richard is a prolific winner of horse trials both here and abroad*

# Kim Walnes (USA)

Kim Walnes (25.2.48), from Woodbury, Connecticut, showed fine form in the trials for the 1982 World Championships and was chosen to make her team debut in Luhmühlen. She and The Gray Goose justified selection by taking the individual bronze, also helping her team to take third place. They had won two of the trials, including that at Lexington where, in 1981, she had finished second. She and The Gray Goose were equal second with eventual winners Lucinda Green and Regal Realm after the speed and endurance phase of the 1982 World Championships, but dropped to third when they hit one show-jumping fence.

# John Watson (Ireland)

John Watson (3.2.52) was born in London but lives in, and rides for, Ireland. He started riding when he was twelve, hunts regularly with the Tipperary Foxhounds, and began eventing in 1969. He and Cambridge Blue were in the Irish squad at the European Championships in 1975 and finished eleventh, but the following year, in Bromont for the Montreal Olympics, Cambridge Blue injured himself on some bad ground while exercising. They were the only Irish competitors in the 1978 World Championships, in Lexington, Kentucky, but won the individual silver, and the following season helped their team win the European Championship for the first time, in Luhmühlen, when they were also placed fifth individually. After a disagreement with the selectors, Watson was dropped from the team that went to Fontainebleau in 1980.

# Jim Wofford (USA)

Jim Wofford (3.11.44), one of a family of noted horsemen from Virginia, has been one of the United States' top internationals for nearly two decades. He took the Irish-bred Kilkenny back to Punchestown for the 1970 World Championships and won the individual bronze medal, and two years later in Munich was a member of the team that took the silver behind Britain, finishing thirtieth individually. He bought Carawich, on which Aly Pattinson had won Burghley in 1975 and was fifth at Badminton in 1977, was tenth on him in the 1978 World Championships in Lexington and second in the 'Alternative Olympics' at Fontainebleau in 1980.

*Meeting everything right, Jim Wofford and Carawich during the show-jumping phase of an international event*

# Appendix
# Championship Results

## Olympic Games

### 1912 Stockholm
*Team*
1 Sweden
2 Germany
3 USA
*Individual*
1 Lieutenant Axel Nordlander (Sweden) Lady Artist
2 Oberleutnant Harry von Rochow (Germany) Idealist
3 Captain Jean Cariou (France) Cocotte

### 1920 Antwerp
*Team*
1 Sweden
2 Italy
3 Belgium
*Individual*
1 Lieutenant Count Helmer Morner (Sweden) Germania
2 Lieutenant Age Lundstrom (Sweden) Yrsa
3 Major Ettore Caffaratti (Italy) Caniche

### 1924 Paris
*Team*
1 Netherlands
2 Sweden
3 Italy

*Individual*
1 Lieutenant A. van der Voort van Zijp (Netherlands) Silver Piece
2 Lieutenant Frode Kirkebjerg (Denmark) Metoo
3 Major Sloan Doak (USA) Pathfinder

### 1928 Amsterdam
*Team*
1 Netherlands
2 Norway
3 Poland
*Individual*
1 Lieutenant Charles F. Pahud de Mortanges (Netherlands) Marcroix
2 Captain Gerard P. de Kruyff (Netherlands) Va-t-en
3 Major Bruno Neumann (Germany) Ilja

### 1932 Los Angeles
*Team*
1 USA
2 Netherlands
Only two teams finished
*Individual*
1 Lieutenant Charles F. Pahud de Mortanges (Netherlands) Marcroix
2 Lieutenant Earl F. Thomson (USA) Jenny Camp
3 Lieutenant Count Clarence von Rosen (Sweden) Sunnyside Maid

### 1936 Berlin
*Team*
1 Germany
2 Poland
3 Great Britain
*Individual*
1 Captain Ludwig Stubbendorf (Germany) Nurmi
2 Captain Earl F. Thomson (USA) Jenny Camp
3 Captain H.M. Lunding (Denmark) Jason

### 1948 London
*Team*
1 USA
2 Sweden
3 Mexico
*Individual*
1 Captain Bernard Chevallier (France) Aiglonne
2 Lieutenant Colonel Frank Henry (USA) Swing Low
3 Captain J. Robert Selfelt (Sweden) Claque

### 1952 Helsinki
*Team*
1 Sweden
2 W. Germany
3 USA

*Individual*
1   Hans von Blixen-Finecke
    (Sweden) Jubal
2   Guy Lefrant (France) Verdun
3   Willi Büsing (W. Germany)
    Hubertus

### 1956 Stockholm

*Team*
1   Great Britain
2   W. Germany
3   Canada
*Individual*
1   Petrus Kastenmann (Sweden)
    Illuster
2   August Lütke-Westhues
    (W. Germany) Trux von Kamax
3   Lieutenant Colonel Frank Weldon
    (GB) Kilbarry

### 1960 Rome

*Team*
1   Australia
2   Switzerland
3   France
*Individual*
1   Laurence Morgan (Australia)
    Salad Days
2   Neale Lavis (Australia)
    Mirrabooka
3   Anton Bühler (Switzerland)
    Gay Spark

### 1964 Tokyo

*Team*
1   Italy
2   USA
3   W. Germany
*Individual*
1   Mauro Checcoli (Italy) Surbean
2   Carlos Moratorio (Argentina)
    Chalan
3   Fritz Ligges (W. Germany)
    Donkosak

### 1968 Mexico

*Team*
1   Great Britain
2   USA
3   Australia
*Individual*
1   Jean-Jacques Guyon (France) Pitou
2   Major Derek Allhusen (GB)
    Lochinvar
3   Michael Page (USA) Foster

### 1972 Munich

*Team*
1   Great Britain
2   USA
3   W. Germany
*Individual*
1   Richard Meade (GB) Laurieston
2   Alessandro Argenton (Italy)
    Woodland
3   Jan Jonsson (Sweden) Sarajevo

### 1976 Montreal

*Team*
1   USA
2   W. Germany
3   Australia
*Individual*
1   Tad Coffin (USA) Ballycor
2   Michael Plumb (USA) Better and
    Better
3   Karl Schultz (Germany) Madrigal

### 1980 Moscow

*Team*
1   USSR
2   Italy
3   Mexico
*Individual*
1   Federico Euro Roman (Italy)
    Rossinan
2   Alexandre Blinov (USSR) Galzun
3   Yuri Salnikov (USSR) Pintset

### Fontainebleau Festival 1980 ('Alternative Olympics')

*Team*
1   France
2   W. Germany
3   Australia
*Individual*
1   Nils Haagensen (Denmark)
    Monaco
2   James Wofford (USA) Carawich
3   Torrance Watkins (USA)
    Poltroon

# World Championships

### 1966 Burghley

*Team*
1   Ireland
2   Argentina
Only two teams finished

*Individual*
1   Captain Carlos Moratorio
    (Argentina) Chalan
2   Richard Meade (GB) Barberry
3   Miss Virginia Freeman-Jackson
    (Ireland) Sam Weller

### 1970 Punchestown

*Team*
1   Great Britain
2   France
Only two teams finished
*Individual*
1   Miss Mary Gordon-Watson (GB)
    Cornishman V
2   Richard Meade (GB) The Poacher
3   James Wofford (USA) Kilkenny

### 1974 Burghley

*Team*
1   USA
2   Great Britain
3   W. Germany
*Individual*
1   Bruce Davidson (USA) Irish Cap
2   Michael Plumb (USA) Good
    Mixture
3   Hugh Thomas (GB) Playamar

### 1978 Lexington

*Team*
1   Canada
2   W. Germany
3   USA
*Individual*
1   Bruce Davidson (USA) Might
    Tango
2   John Watson (Ireland) Cambridge
    Blue
3   Helmut Rethemeier (W. Germany)
    Ladalco

### 1982 Luhmühlen

*Team*
1   Great Britain
2   W. Germany
3   USA
*Individual*
1   Mrs Lucinda Green (GB) Regal
    Realm
2   Helmut Rethemeier (W. Germany)
    Santiago
3   Miss Kim Walnes (USA) The
    Gray Goose

# European Championships

## 1953 Badminton
*Team*
1 Great Britain
No other team finished
*Individual*
1 Major Lawrence Rook (GB)
  Starlight XV
2 Major Frank Weldon (GB)
  Kilbarry
3 Captain Hans Schwarzenbach
  (Switzerland) Vae Victis

## 1954 Basle
*Team*
1 Great Britain
2 W. Germany
Only two teams finished
*Individual*
1 Bertie Hill (GB) Crispin
2 Major Frank Weldon (GB)
  Kilbarry
3 Major Lawrence Rook (GB)
  Starlight XV

## 1955 Windsor
*Team*
1 Great Britain
2 Switzerland
Only two teams finished
*Individual*
1 Major Frank Weldon (GB)
  Kilbarry
2 Lieutenant Commander John
  Oram (GB) Radar
3 Bertie Hill (GB) Countryman

## 1957 Copenhagen
*Team*
1 Great Britain
2 W. Germany
3 Sweden
*Individual*
1 Miss Sheila Willcox (GB) High
  and Mighty
2 August Lütke-Westhues
  (W. Germany) Franko
3 J. Lindgren (Sweden) Eldorado

## 1959 Harewood
*Team*
1 W.Germany
2 Great Britain
3 France

*Individual*
1 Major Hans Schwarzenbach
  (Switzerland) Burn Trout
2 Lieutenant Colonel Frank Weldon
  (GB) Samuel Johnson
3 Major Derek Allhusen (GB)
  Laurien

## 1962 Burghley
*Team*
1 USSR
2 Ireland
3 Great Britain
*Individual*
1 Captain James Templer (GB)
  M'Lord Connolly
2 G. Gazumov (USSR) Granj
3 Miss Jane Wykeham-Musgrave
  (GB) Ryebrooks

## 1965 Moscow
*Team*
1 USSR
2 Ireland
3 Great Britain
*Individual*
1 Marian Babirecki (Poland) Volt
2 Lew Baklyshkin (USSR) Ruon
3 Horst Karsten (W. Germany)
  Condora

## 1967 Punchestown
*Team*
1 Great Britain
2 Ireland
3 France
*Individual*
1 Major Eddie Boylan (Ireland)
  Durlas Eile
2 Martin Whiteley (GB) The
  Poacher
3 Major Derek Allhusen (GB)
  Lochinvar

## 1969 Haras du Pin
*Team*
1 Great Britain
2 USSR
3 W. Germany
*Individual*
1 Miss Mary Gordon-Watson (GB)
  Cornishman V
2 Richard Walker (GB) Pasha
3 Bernd Messmann (W. Germany)
  Windspiel

## 1971 Burghley
*Team*
1 Great Britain
2 USSR
3 W. Germany
*Individual*
1 HRH Princess Anne (GB)
  Doublet
2 Miss Debbie West (GB) Baccarat
3 Stewart Stevens (GB) Classic
  Chips

## 1973 Kiev
*Team*
1 W. Germany
2 USSR
3 Great Britain
*Individual*
1 Alexandre Evdokimov (USSR)
  Jeger
2 Herbert Blöcker (W. Germany)
  Albrant
3 Horst Karsten (W. Germany)
  Sioux

## 1975 Luhmühlen
*Team*
1 USSR
2 Great Britain
3 W. Germany
*Individual*
1 Miss Lucinda Prior-Palmer (GB)
  Be Fair
2 HRH Princess Anne (GB)
  Goodwill
3 Peter Gornuschko (USSR) Gusar

## 1977 Burghley
*Team*
1 Great Britain
2 W. Germany
3 Ireland
*Individual*
1 Miss Lucinda Prior-Palmer (GB)
  George
2 Karl Schultz (W. Germany)
  Madrigal
3 Horst Karsten (W. Germany)
  Sioux

## 1979 Luhmühlen
*Team*
1 Ireland
2 Great Britain
3 France

*Individual*
1  Nils Haagensen (Denmark) Monaco
2  Miss Rachel Bayliss (GB) Gurgle the Greek
3  Rudiger Schwarz (W. Germany) Power Game

### 1981 Horsens
*Team*
1  Great Britain
2  Switzerland
3  Poland
*Individual*
1  Hansueli Schmutz (Switzerland) Oran
2  Helmut Rethemeier (W. Germany) Santiago
3  Brian MacSweeny (Ireland) Inis Meain

### 1983 Frauenfeld
*Team*
1  Sweden
2  Great Britain
3  France
*Individual*
1  Miss Rachel Bayliss (GB) Mystic Minstrel
2  Mrs Lucinda Green (GB) Regal Realm
3  Christian Persson (Sweden) Joel

# European Junior Championships

### 1967 Eridge
*Team*
No team contest
*Individual*
1  A. Souchon (France) Roi d'Asturie
2  R. Walker (GB) Pasha
3  P. Giraud (France) Saphir d'Eau

### 1968 Craon
*Team*
1  France
2  Great Britain
3  Poland
*Individual*
1  R. Walker (GB) Pasha
2  P. Giraud (France) Gallax
3  A. Sarrant (France) Palestro

### 1969 Euskirchen
*Team*
1  USSR
2  France
3  W. Germany
*Individual*
1  H.-O. Bolten (W.Germany) Lansbub XIII
2  V. Tichkin (USSR) Elion
3  Miss A. Pattinson (GB) Sharon

### 1970 Holstebro
*Team*
1  W. Germany
2  France
3  Great Britain
*Individual*
1  N.-O. Barkander (Sweden) Pegasus
2  A. Fenner (W. Germany) Anemone
3  B. Wahler (W. Germany) Marcus IV

### 1971 Wesel
*Team*
1  Great Britain
2  France
3  USSR
*Individual*
1  C. Brooke (GB) Olive Oyl
2  F. Lault (France) Un de la Côte
3  S. Nikolski (USSR) Vostorg

### 1972 Eridge
*Team*
1  Great Britain
2  France
3  Netherlands
*Individual*
1  B. Clement (France) Quel Pich
2  A. Hill (GB) Maid Marion
3  G. Heyligers (Netherlands) Full Speed

### 1973 Pompadour
*Team*
1  Great Britain
2  Italy
3  Ireland
*Individual*
1  Miss V. Holgate (GB) Dubonnet
2  Miss S. Bailey (GB) Red Amber
3  A. Miserocchi (Italy) Friday

### 1974 Rome
*Team*
1  W. Germany
2  Ireland
3  USSR
*Individual*
1  Miss S. Ker (GB) Peer Gynt
2  T. Esteve (France) Urgel
3  Miss J. Winter (GB) Stainless Steel

### 1975
*No championships held*

### 1976 Siekkrug
*Team*
1  Great Britain
2  France
3  Italy
*Individual*
1  O. Depagne (France) Bobineau
2  Miss D. Saffell (GB) Double Brandy
3  Miss S. Bouet (GB) Sea Lord V

### 1977 Fontainebleau
*Team*
1  Ireland
2  W. Germany
3  Poland
*Individual*
1  M. Spehmann (W. Germany) Lorbass
2  P. Cronier (France) Dandy XXVI
3  M. Otto (W. Germany) Pergola

### 1978 Burghley
*Team*
1  W. Germany
2  France
3  Ireland
*Individual*
1  D. Baumgart (W Germany) Kurfurst
2  R. Ehrenbrink (W. Germany) Huntsman
3  P. Cronier (France) Danseur II

### 1979 Punchestown
*Team*
1  France
2  Great Britain
3  Ireland
*Individual*
1  Miss N. May (GB) Commodore IV
2  J. Dermody (Ireland) Heathcliffe
3  M. Sebilleau (France) Dragomiroff

## 1980 Achselschwang
*Team*
1 Great Britain
2 Sweden
3 France
*Individual*
1 Miss C. Berger (W. Germany) Bacardi
2 Miss C. Needham (GB) Solo
3 R. Funder (Austria) Dac

## 1981 St Fargeau
*Team*
1 France
2 Great Britain
3 Italy
*Individual*
1 O. Guelin (France) Isa E
2 T. Kapsareit (W. Germany) Tamino
3 C. Pic (France) Horison de Juis

## 1982 Rotherfield
*Team*
1 Great Britain
2 Poland
3 France

*Individual*
1 Miss K. Straker (GB) Running Bear
2 C. Pic (France) Horison de Juis
3 A. Osica (Poland) Hel

## 1983 Rome
*Team*
1 Great Britain
2 Italy
3 France
*Individual*
1 Miss H. Brown (GB) Fleetwood Opposition
2 Miss L. Vitali (Italy) Clever P
3 L. Koenig (France) Hardy Petit

# European Young Riders' Championships

## 1981 Achselschwang
*Team*
1 Great Britain
2 France
3 Poland

*Individual*
1 O. Depagne (France) Destrier
2 Miss S. Kronenberg (W. Germany) Flicka 30
3 D. Hogrefe (W. Germany) Foliant 6

## 1982 Fontainebleau
*Team*
1 W. Germany
2 Great Britain
3 Austria
*Individual*
1 Miss V. Strawson (GB) Minsmore
2 V. Wippel (Austria) Rigoletto
3 O. Depagne (France) Destrier

## 1983 Burghley
*Team*
1 Great Britain
2 France
3 Ireland
*Individual*
1 J. P. Saint Vignes (France) Jocelyn A
2 Miss K. Straker (GB) Running Bear
3 Miss P. Schwerdt (GB) Dylan

# Badminton

1949 J. Shedden (GB) Golden Willow
1950 Captain J. A. Collings (GB) Remus
1951 Captain H. Schwarzenbach (Switzerland) Vae Victis
1952 Captain M. A. Q. Darley (GB) Emily Little
1953 European Championships
1954 Miss M. Hough (GB) Bambi V
1955 No competition
1956 Major F. W. C. Weldon (GB) Kilbarry
1957 Miss S. Willcox (GB) High and Mighty
1958 Miss S. Willcox (GB) High and Mighty
1959 Mrs S. Waddington (née Willcox) (GB) Airs and Graces
1960 W. Roycroft (Australia) Our Solo
1961 L. Morgan (Australia) Salad Days
1962 Miss A. Drummond-Hay (GB) Merely-a-Monarch
1963 Cancelled
1964 Captain J. R. Templer (GB) M'Lord Connolly
1965 Major E. A. Boylan (Ireland) Durlas Eile
1966 Cancelled

1967 Miss C. Ross-Taylor (GB) Jonathan
1968 Miss J. Bullen (GB) Our Nobby
1969 R. Walker (GB) Pasha
1970 R. Meade (GB) The Poacher
1971 Lieutenant M. Phillips (GB) Great Ovation
1972 Lieutenant M. Phillips (GB) Great Ovation
1973 Miss L. Prior-Palmer (GB) Be Fair
1974 Captain M. Phillips (GB) Columbus
1975 Cancelled after dressage
1976 Miss L. Prior-Palmer (GB) Wide Awake
1977 Miss L. Prior-Palmer (GB) George
1978 Mrs T. Holderness-Roddam (née Bullen) (GB) Warrior
1979 Miss L. Prior-Palmer (GB) Killaire
1980 M. Todd (New Zealand) Southern Comfort
1981 Captain M. Phillips (GB) Lincoln
1982 R. Meade (GB) Speculator III
1983 Mrs D. Green (née Prior-Palmer) (GB) Regal Realm

# Burghley

| | |
|---|---|
| 1961 | Miss A. Drummond-Hay (GB) Merely-a-Monarch |
| 1962 | European Championships |
| 1963 | Captain H. Freeman-Jackson (Ireland) St Finnbarr |
| 1964 | R. Meade (GB) Barberry |
| 1965 | Captain J. J. Beale (GB) Victoria Bridge |
| 1966 | World Championships |
| 1967 | Miss L. Sutherland (GB) Popadom |
| 1968 | Miss S. Willcox (GB) Fair and Square |
| 1969 | Miss G. Watson (GB) Shaitan |
| 1970 | Miss J. Bradwell (GB) Don Camillo |
| 1971 | European Championships |
| 1972 | Miss J. Hodgson (GB) Larkspur |
| 1973 | Captain M. Phillips (GB) Maid Marion |
| 1974 | World Championships |
| 1975 | Miss A. Pattinson (GB) Carawich |
| 1976 | Mrs T. Holderness-Roddam (GB) Warrior |
| 1977 | European Championships |
| 1978 | Mrs L. Clarke (née Sutherland) (GB) Greco |
| 1979 | A. Hoy (Australia) Davey |
| 1980 | R. Walker (GB) John o' Gaunt |
| 1981 | Miss L. Prior-Palmer (GB) Beagle Bay |
| 1982 | R. Walker (GB) Ryan's Cross |
| 1983 | Miss V. Holgate (GB) Priceless |

# Photograph Acknowledgements

*Black and white:* Frontispiece, Kit Houghton; page 10, Kit Houghton; page 11, Kit Houghton; page 12 above, Kit Houghton; page 12 below, Kit Houghton; page 13, Kit Houghton; page 14, Kit Houghton; page 15, Colorsport; page 18, Jim Meads; pages 20/1, Colorsport; page 22, Kit Houghton; page 25, E. D. Lacey; page 26, Popperfoto; page 29, Kit Houghton; page 30, Jim Meads; page 33 above, Peter Harding; page 33 below, Fox Photos; page 34 above, BBC Hulton Picture Library; page 34 below, Peter Harding; page 35, Peter Harding; page 36, Peter Ayres; page 37, Peter Harding; pages 38/9 (*left to right*) above, All-Sport, Steve Yarnell, Colorsport, below, Kit Houghton, Peter Ayres; pages 40/1 sequence, Steve Yarnell; page 41 right, Kit Houghton; page 42, Stuart Newsham; page 43, Steve Yarnell; pages 44/5 sequence, Colorsport; pages 46/7 (*left to right*) above, E. D. Lacey, Jim Meads, below, Jim Meads, All-Sport; page 48, Kit Houghton; page 50, Colorsport; page 51, Kit Houghton; page 52, Kit Houghton; page 53 above, Stuart Newsham; page 53 below, Kit Houghton; page 54, All-Sport; page 55, Colorsport; page 56, Jim Meads; page 57, Kit Houghton; page 58, Findlay Davidson; page 60, Kit Houghton; page 61 left, Kit Houghton; page 61 right, Kit Houghton; page 62, Jim Meads; page 63 above, Colorsport; page 63 below, Kit Houghton; page 64, Kit Houghton; page 65, Steve Yarnell; page 66 left, Jim Meads; page 66 right, Stuart Newsham; page 67, Keystone Press Agency; pages 68/9, Steve Yarnell; page 70 above, Kit Houghton; page 70 below, Kit Houghton; page 71, Leslie Lane; page 72, Jim Meads; page 73, Jim Meads; page 74 above, Jim Meads; page 74 below, All-Sport; page 75 above, Kit Houghton; page 75 below, Kit Houghton; page 77, Colorsport; page 79, Press Association; page 80, Jim Meads; page 82, All-Sport; page 84, Colorsport; page 85, Stuart Newsham; page 87, Kit Houghton; page 88, Keystone Press Agency; page 89, Fox Photos; page 92, Findlay Davidson; page 95, Kit Houghton; page 97, Jim Meads; page 98, Jim Meads; page 99 Kit Houghton; page 100, Kit Houghton; page 101, Steve Yarnell; page 102, Stuart Newsham; pages 104/5, Kit Houghton; page 107, Pressens Bild AB; page 108, BBC Hulton Picture Library; page 109 above, BBC Hulton Picture Library; page 109 below, Central Press Photos Ltd; page 110, Pressens Bild AB; page 111 above, Keystone Press Agency; page 111 below, Keystone Press Agency; page 112 above, Popperfoto; page 112 below, Keystone Press Agency; page 113, Central Press Photos Ltd; page 114 above, Popperfoto; page 114 below, Popperfoto; page 115, Popperfoto; page 116, Popperfoto; page 117, Keystone Press Agency; page 118, Popperfoto; page 119, Popperfoto; page 121, Syndication International; page 122, Keystone Press Agency; page 123, Popperfoto; page 124 above, Four Footed Fotos; page 124 below, Four Footed Fotos; page 125, Jim Meads; pages 128/9, Leslie Lane; page 130, Kit Houghton; page 132, Kit Houghton; page 133 above, Kit Houghton; page 133 below, Kit Houghton; page 134, Camera Press; page 135, Leslie Lane; page 136, Jim Meads; page 137, Eamonn McCabe; page 138, Camera Press; page 139, Kit Houghton; page 140 left, Peter Harding; pages 140/1 sequence, Findlay Davidson; page 142, John Scott; page 143, Jim Meads; page 145, Kit Houghton; pages 146/7 sequence, Findlay Davidson; page 147 below, Kit Houghton; page 151 left, Kit Houghton; page 151 right, Findlay Davidson;